PEBBLE CLLECTING & PLISHING

By Edward Fletcher

STERLING PUBLISHING CO., INC.   NEW YORK

Edited and adapted for the American audience by
Joe Rothstein

Photographs by Michael Allman and Joe Rothstein
Drawings by John Wood

Acknowledgments

The author and publisher wish to thank the following for their assistance: Gemrocks Ltd., London; Roland Phelps for supplying the pebbles in Illus. 19, 20, 24, and the fossil in Illus. 47; British Travel for Illus. 13; Institute of Geological Sciences (Crown Copyright) for Illus. 33.

American edition © 1973 by Sterling Publishing Co., Inc., 419 Park Avenue South, New York, New York 10016. Originally published in Great Britain under the title "Pebble Polishing" © 1972 by Blandford Press Ltd.
Manufactured in the United States of America   *All rights reserved*
Library of Congress Catalog Card No.: 72-95210
ISBN 0-8069-3054-3
3055-1

Contents

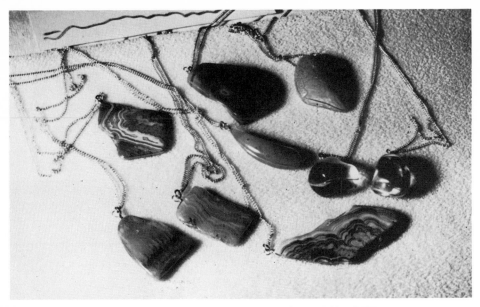

Illus. 1. Tumble-polished pebbles mounted on findings.

Before You Begin

Pebble collecting, which was well known in our grandparents' day as a casual pastime for those infrequent one-day visits to the seaside, has come back into fashion lately in a big way. At the same time it has developed into a creative, absorbing occupation for the hobbyist, offering tremendous personal pleasure and satisfaction.

Mass production of cheap costume jewelry has enjoyed a boom in recent years. Millions of dollars are spent annually on rings, bracelets, pendants, baubles and beads manufactured from colored glass and plastics and sold in chain stores all over the country. The discerning woman, anxious to acquire something different, something unique in costume jewelry, finds little to satisfy her tastes in a market where 90 per cent of the goods are of a very low standard.

It is to fill this gap that thousands of women (and not a few men) have seized on pebble collecting and tumble-polishing as a means of making their own unique and beautiful jewelry. Unlike their grand-mothers, who relied on skilled lapidaries to transform their finds into gems, today's collectors can polish and mount their pebbles easily, quickly and at little expense. This has been made possible thanks to the recent introduction of tumble-polishing machines, epoxy resin and inexpensive jewelry findings, all of which are extremely simple to use.

To work efficiently, a tumble-polisher requires nothing more than connection to the household electricity, some pebbles, a suitable abrasive grit or polish and ordinary tap water. It will transform humble beach pebbles into highly polished gems with the minimum

Illus. 2. Collecting on Obsidian Cliffs, along the Yellowstone River.

of care and attention. Epoxy resin is simply strong, permanent glue, and modern jewelry findings come in a wide variety of shapes and sizes, catering to every taste. With a little patience and artistic flair, anyone can make jewelry of the highest quality.

Of course, the other great attraction of the hobby is that it combines outdoor fun with indoor pleasure. Collecting the pebbles is as exciting as making the jewelry. Beaches abound with beautiful stones; amethysts, carnelians, jaspers, agates, milky quartz and serpentine can all be found quite readily at a hundred and one different holiday locations. Whole summers can be spent in happy and successful hunting—perhaps beachcombing Oregon's shoreline for agate, the rocky coast of northern Maine for jasper, or the inland dunes of Lake Superior for lovely, pastel agates. Or, more likely, simply collecting some of the countless millions of more humble yet just as colorful pebbles which attract the eye on almost every beach in America.

Detailed knowledge of geology is not necessary to make pebble collecting and polishing worthwhile. Knowing a few simple rules—and what *not* to collect—is all that is required. Collecting the pebbles will almost certainly stimulate a desire for a greater knowledge and it will not be long before a newcomer to the hobby begins to recognize most of his finds. With this knowledge will come deep appreciation of this truly fascinating subject and its possibilities.

The purpose of this book is to take the beginner step by step through every stage in baroque jewelry-making: where to find the pebbles, which ones to collect, buying a tumbler, achieving first-class results when polishing, and how to mount the polished stones on findings. In addition, the time will certainly come when you will want to polish some of the exotic stones which are now imported into the United States from all over the world, for example tiger's eye, malachite, or rhodochrosite; or try your hand at grinding, cutting or even faceting stones. Finally, there is a section devoted to current magazines of the hobby where lapidary and jewelry-findings suppliers advertise and the latest in machines and equipment can be selected.

Illus. 3. Beaches, brooks, lake shores—all abound with suitable pebbles for your polishing.

1. Where the Pebbles Are

No matter where you live in America, some sort of collecting is possible. Almost anywhere is good, but there are certain locations which are better than others. The aim here is to give you a gentle push in the direction of those better sites.

Most of us like variety and that is just what the best locations have— a wide variety of colorful and beautiful pebbles which are yours for the taking. While the West abounds in agate locations, other sections have good areas. The secret is in knowing where to look. Nature has shared her prizes so well that anyone should be able to reach at least one really outstanding area and return home with all the pebbles he or she can carry within a day or a weekend trip. You can, if you wish, take a pebble-hunting holiday without forfeiting good hotels, food or entertainment.

Some Ideas of Where to Collect

There are so many collecting areas in the United States and Canada that only a few of the famous ones are given here for a beginning. Every beach, every stream, every creek where there is a gravel bar is a place to look. Collecting in Mexico is generally not allowed—that government feels it is a source of revenue for its low-income groups and frowns on alien collectors removing gem minerals that villagers can gather and sell.

The best place? While the shoreline of the entire Pacific Coast is a treasure house, the finest beachcombing in the United States is on the Oregon coast. The highway parallels the shore, state parks are numerous, and always there are agates. After a storm when new gravels are exposed, the pickings are good. Besides, there is something for the whole family—driftwood everywhere, fossil pebbles on the middle beaches—once during your lifetime, you should make the trip.

Illus. 4. The Oregon coast is a pebble collector's paradise.

Illus. 5. The whole family (including the baby) can enjoy pebble collecting.

If you visit Hearst's Castle at San Simeon in Southern California, check the beach there and just north of the town of Cambria. At San Simeon back from the beach in the sand banks, jasper pebbles provide happy collecting. In San Francisco, at Land's End, a small cove near the Golden Gate bridge, there are plenty of jasper pebbles on the beach.

These collecting areas, as well as many others, are delineated in the "Western Gem Hunters Atlas," written and published by Cy Johnson, Box 288, Susanville, California. The book is obtainable at most rock shops west of the Mississippi and at most rock shops elsewhere in the United States and Canada. Use it as a guide, but do not be afraid to explore *any* accessible beach or stream. Gravels are brought many miles downstream from their source and tumbled along the way to boot.

In the Midwest, the pastel agates of the Lake Superior region are the lure. Beachcombing is one of the hobbies in Michigan's Upper Peninsula and in Minnesota. Agates can be found on the shore at Marquette, and also on the Keweenaw Peninsula which juts out

Illus. 6. The Keweenaw Peninsula on Lake Superior has agates to offer to the collector.

into Lake Superior nearby, at Copper Harbor and Eagle Harbor. On the east shore of Lake Michigan between Charlevoix and Petoskey there are beaches where the fossilized coral, coelenterata hexagonia, may be found. These corals have been changed to limestone and as the name indicates, form beautiful hexagonal designs. Instead of buying

Illus. 7. Peggy's Cove in Nova Scotia.

the "Petoskey stones" in the tourist shops—find them yourself on the beaches, tumble them, and make your own jewelry (see Illus. 23).

In the East, the northern coasts of Maine are the hunting grounds for the pebble polishers. In the Bar Harbor area (not in Acadia National Park) look for a green, silvery, pebble. It is amazonite of the feldspar family and it can be found on the beaches along with the many pink, granite pebbles. The pink in the granite of the Bar Harbor area is also a feldspar. You cannot collect in Acadia National Park, or any national park for that matter. Mt. Cadillac which overlooks the town of Bar Harbor is composed entirely of pink granite—drive up, admire the view, but no collecting! North of Bar Harbor there are agate and jasper pebble beaches—such as Jasper Beach at Bucks Harbor near Machias. One shop in Bar Harbor makes a specialty of polishing individual pebbles that the casual tourist finds.

Still further north, Nova Scotia takes over. There are accessible beaches near Parrsboro, which is a well known mineral-collecting area. On Cape Blomiden, which may be a little rugged in spots, amethyst

Illus. 8. West Bay near Parrsboro, Nova Scotia, is one of many beaches in the area well known to pebble hunters.

Illus. 9. Ballast Point on Hillsborough Bay in Florida is accessible at low tide when collectors can search without violating private property.

has been found. Both amethyst and agate occur between Kentville and Scott's Bay. There are also agates on the beach just north of the ferry landing at Digby. When exploring on the beaches on the Bay of Fundy, watch the tides. Never let children wander off alone to a beach which is backed up by a steep cliff. It's very easy to forget to watch for the incoming tide.

The South is not so fortunate—most beachcombing turns up shells. However, if you are careful, these too can be tumble-polished and used in baroque jewelry. The one prolific spot was in Florida where carnelian and agate pseudomorphs after coral could once be obtained at Hillsborough Bay which is part of the larger Tampa Bay. It is at the east end of the St. Petersburg-Tampa causeway. Now, it is all private property and pretty much closed to the casual collector. Collecting there becomes quite complicated. However, the tumbling material in the rock shops there is not too expensive, and worth purchasing for your own jewelry. Wherever dredges are at work in Florida, explore a little, and sometimes you will find surprises such as massive, golden calcite.

There are river localities in the Southwest worthy of mention. Moss agate and jasper pebbles can be found in an area forty miles up and down the Rio Grande from Laredo, Texas, but the most famous moss agate river location is along the Yellowstone River at Glendive, Montana.

Never think everything is picked over—there are more pebbles weathering out of the rocks now than ever came out!

These are only a few of the well known areas, but every local club has its spots. The terminal moraine beaches around Wildwood State Park on the North Shore of Long Island yield a good variety of pebbles, so that even in a well populated area, there is good collecting.

Clubs in the United States and Canada not only welcome newcomers, they fuss over them. Most conduct regular field trips as part of the activities and a good many publish maps of collecting areas in their region. While many of the field trips may be too rough and dangerous for a family excursion, there is always a spot or two where you can take the family for a picnic and hunt for pebbles. Because it is accessible, most of the members of the club will have collected there and will be blasé about the collecting, but go anyway—you'll have a good time even if you don't make a great "find."

Illus. 10. The terminal moraine beaches on the North Shore of Long Island offer a wide selection, including pebbles of New England origin.

Illus. 11. Basic equipment for collecting.

Equipment for Collecting

There cannot be many hobbies which require so little outlay on equipment as pebble collecting. True, you need a tumble-polishing machine if you are going to polish your finds when you get them home, but the basic raw materials—pebbles—are yours for the taking. You can get by with a pocket handkerchief or a brown paper bag if you find yourself with half an hour to spare on an unexpected visit to the coast. However, several basic items—all of which are certain to be lying around at home—are well worth taking on any expedition. They are:

three small plastic bags to put your pebbles in;
a penknife with a strong blade;
a small steel file.

For most people collecting pebbles is a family activity, with Dad, Mother, the children and even the family dog joining in, so three bags are not so unmanageable as they sound. In the next chapter you will find how you can group your pebbles in a way which will help you achieve the best results when you go on to polishing. As this grouping can be done during collecting with the aid of your penknife and file, and as you will be placing your pebbles into one of three groups, you can complete the job on the beach by putting each pebble into one of your three bags. Or if you go on your own, you can make do with one large bag and carry out the grouping at home.

The best part of the beach to search for pebbles of a suitable size for your tumbler is down by the water's edge, so it is wise to wear an old pair of sandals or sneakers. And do not forget to take a warm sweater or jacket, even in summertime. You might spend a couple of hours combing the beach for the pebbles you need and sea breezes can be quite cold no matter how blue the sky. And in the states of Oregon and Washington, keep a raincoat handy.

Safety

There is nothing dangerous about pebble collecting. The only possible risk arises from the fact that looking for pebbles is such an absorbing pastime that you might forget that tides come in as often as they go out. On some coasts the tide can sweep in with treacherous speed, so do keep an eye on the sea—especially on any beach backed by cliffs. If there is no way out of an interesting cove up the cliffside, make certain that you give yourself ample time to walk to safety before the tide comes in. The local Coast Guard is only a telephone call away and can give you reliable information about how long you can safely spend on such beaches. In the Bay of Fundy area, especially, take no chances.

Remember, too, that steep cliffs can hold other dangers. Confine your searching to the beach, well away from the cliff face where rock falls could lead to disaster.

Illus. 12. Watch that tide! Never allow yourself to get stranded on a beach backed up by cliffs, and keep your eye on wandering children.

Illus. 13.

2.   Selecting Your Pebbles

Happily, it is quite unnecessary to possess a detailed knowledge of geology or mineralogy to collect pebbles that will polish well and make up into beautiful jewelry. Nevertheless, the question on every beginner's lips is, "How do I know which pebbles to collect?" The practical answer is to learn half a dozen basic rules which will help you to eliminate pebbles quite useless for tumble-polishing and to collect suitable ones which attract or please your eye. You *will* make mistakes and your first attempts at polishing are unlikely to be first-class. But you will learn far more by this trial-and-error method than any reference book could ever teach you.

To the perfectionist this may sound like sidestepping the question. For those who would like to go further into it, a course in mineralogy and gemology and the books on page 94 are recommended. In a couple of years you will have learned a great deal about the subject and no doubt have your own views on tumbling. Meanwhile, readers who follow our simpler method of identification will find that their final results are just as good as the results of those who decide to study the subject scientifically.

The Basic Rules

SIZE. Always collect small pebbles. Larger ones make excellent doorstops, paperweights, and ballast but they do not tumble. Look for pebbles between the size of your smallest fingernail and the top joint of your thumb. One or two slightly larger ones may be included if they are particularly worth having, but bear in mind that your ultimate aim is to make jewelry. You require pebbles suitably sized for earrings, bracelets, necklaces and rings.

Do not make the mistake of collecting pebbles of uniform size. Aim at a good selection between the smallest and largest. Tumblers work more efficiently when loaded with pebbles of different sizes and you will need different sizes when making up your jewelry.

SHAPE. Beginners usually make the mistake of collecting either all near-perfectly round pebbles or only those which look like the work of an adventurous modern sculptor. A happy compromise is what you should aim at. Collect a variety of shapes, but consider their usability as you do so. Weird and wonderful shapes have only a limited use in jewelry-making; whereas ovoids, flat discs, spheres and other uniform shapes are all worth collecting.

AMOUNT. The temptation to collect too many pebbles is often hard to resist—especially when you are on a stretch of beach with an abundant supply of colorful material— but you must learn to discipline yourself. Bear in mind the capacity of your tumbler barrels, the number of jewelry findings you plan to buy, the length of time until your next visit to the coast and the problems of storage at home.

The removal of large quantities of pebbles from beaches may be frowned upon by local authorities. No one will prevent you from taking away a few pounds of pretty pebbles, but if every visitor to the beach went home with a truckload of pebbles, there would be a big hole in the ground!

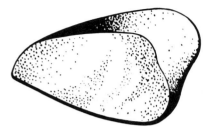

Illus. 14. Sandstone pebbles, both coarse-grained (left) and fine-grained (right) do not polish well.

WHAT TO LEAVE BEHIND. There are far more pebbles on an average beach that will polish than there are pebbles that will not. If you can recognize the ones that will not, you will automatically know the ones that will. Pebbles that will not polish well can all be recognized by their surface appearance and their feel to your fingers. These are the *porous*, the *granular*, the *flaky* and the *veined*; all of them are very soft. Very soft pebbles will not polish in a tumbler. The abrasive power of the grits used in the process is too great; they disintegrate and upset the grinding and polishing sequence in the barrel. (See page 25.)

(a) *The porous.* These can be quickly spotted. They are the pebbles which stay wet too long. You will often find them well above the waterline and still moist when other pebbles nearby are quite dry. The worst ones will crumble under your fingernail; others will feel very coarse to your touch. They are usually sandstone and probably brown or yellow.

(b) *The granular.* These also stay wet too long, and are usually sandstone. They *can* be finely textured but you will probably be able to see the minute grains of sand from which they are formed. They are often collected by beginners because they can be colorful—greens, reds, yellows and browns—but this is simply mineral-oxide staining.

(c) *The flaky.* The parallel layers of material which make up these pebbles are usually readily visible to the naked eye. In certain varieties, known as *slates*, each layer represents a single stage in a long process of formation—the laying down and compressing of clay over millions of years. These layers can be flaked off with the point of a knife.

Others, known as *mudstone,* have even closer parallel layers which have been formed from fine mud and these layers can be difficult to see. A knife blade will scratch such pebbles easily. A third and very large group, the *schists,* have the same characteristic layers but often tempt collectors because they contain other mineral particles which impart pretty colors or attractive sparkle.

(d) *The veined.* These cause much trouble to old hands at the game as well as to beginners. They can be extremely beautiful and the temptation to drop one or two into one of your collecting bags is great. Pale pink, deep red, yellow, white and translucent are the colors found, usually as a swirling tracery of veins in finely textured sandstone pebbles. Examine one closely and you will see that the veins stand above the general surface. This is because they are composed of much harder material—quartz, feldspar, or jasper—and have resisted erosion far better than the sandstone in the main body of the pebble.

There is another very common type of pebble which you should not collect. This is the badly pitted or cracked specimen of *any* variety. A pebble with a deeply pitted surface will take a long time to grind smooth in your tumbler. Other pebbles will be ready for the next stage in the process long before a pitted one has been worn to smoothness and you will almost certainly have to reject it at some stage. A rare or particularly beautiful pebble which has surface blemishes *can* be saved at the expense of size. This is done either by hand-polishing (a long and slow process) or by putting it through a very prolonged first tumbling phase. The pebble is extracted from the load after a barrel is emptied at the end of the first stage and returned to stock to await

Illus. 15. More pebbles to avoid—schist (left) which is flaky, and veined pebbles, such as the slate with quartz veins at the right.

Illus. 16. Searching along a carnelian brook near Sterling, New Jersey. (See page 49.)

the next batch of pebbles going into the barrel for the first time. By doing this three or four times it is possible to wear down the pebble to a point where all surface pitting is removed. It will, however, be greatly reduced in size—a point worth bearing in mind if you are planning to make a piece of jewelry requiring a large pebble. Any badly cracked pebble is likely to fracture during the rugged first stage of tumbling and its sharp edges will not wear down quickly enough to be ready for second-stage grinding at the end of the first run.

The last item on the "leave-it-behind" list is man-made material. There is a surprising amount on most beaches and you should learn to recognize it. Five man-made materials can be confused with pebbles: brick, concrete, earthenware, china and glass. The ceaseless pounding of the waves and the grinding action of sand can wear fragments of these materials to pebble shape in a very short time. Corners are knocked off, surfaces smoothed, colors bleached, and a deceptive coating given to the finished shape. Even mineralogists can be confused. But do not despair: the seeker after pebbles for tumble-polishing is unlikely to be bothered by four of these intruders.

A pebble of brick will be either red or yellow, and when you have examined it closely you will recognize it as brick or else take it for jasper (see page 25) or sandstone. Scratch it with a knife. If it scrapes easily, it is not jasper. You already know that sandstone is unsuitable for polishing and should be rejected. Thus, brick pebbles should present no problem. Pebbles of concrete should also be thrown away.

Earthenware and china are also likely to be taken for sandstone, in which case the above test applies. You might confuse them with shale or mudstone but, once again, you are not interested in collecting either of these.

This leaves us with glass pebbles which, unfortunately, do not look at all like the bottle glass from which they were formed. Whether clear or colored, they will be dramatically changed. All glassiness will have disappeared and they will have a frosted, crystalline appearance. The colored ones are almost certain to be glass, but if you feel lucky break off a tiny fragment with your file. If an obvious glassiness is seen where the fragment has been removed, then glass it is. The colorless pebble could be pure quartz as such pebbles are to be found occasionally on some beaches. In Cape May, New Jersey, they are found in the vicinity of the Coast Guard station and are faceted and sold to the tourists as Cape May "diamonds." You will be unable to break off a fragment with knifeblade or file if it is quartz. In this case take it home, and in a dark room, strike it with the blade of your knife. If it sparks and emits a burning vegetable smell, you have a quartz pebble. A conchoidal, or shell-like, fracture is another indication.

Incidentally, glass pebbles *will* polish in a tumbler if the barrel is filled entirely with such pebbles.

Summary of unsuitable pebbles:
1. Porous sandstone.
2. Granular sandstone.
3. Flaky shale, slate, mudstone or schist.
4. Veined sandstone.
5. Pitted or cracked pebbles.
6. Brick, concrete, earthenware or china.
7. Glass pebbles, unless you load your tumbler with nothing else but these.
8. Finally, remember not to collect overlarge pebbles or pebbles completely regular in size and shape.

Grouping the Pebbles

Now that you know the pebbles to avoid when collecting, we can give some consideration to the pebbles which might end up in one of your bags. Most beginners are attracted to a pebble by its color and this is a fine way to start. It is unnecessary to arrive at a positive identification of each pebble. You need only know its approximate hardness. Bear in mind, however, that pebbles of the same color do not necessarily have the same hardness and the first thing you must do when picking up specimens is to determine the approximate hardness. This is a simple operation. Take your penknife and scrape the pebble's surface. You may find that it has a coating—a crust of whitish lime or red, black or even green oxide. Remove some of this crust until the true surface appears. Now attempt to scratch this exposed area with your blade. If you cannot scratch it, you have a relatively hard pebble which will probably take a good polish. Try marking it with your hard steel file and if this leaves no mark, put it in your "hard" bag.

If your knifeblade does scratch the surface you have a pebble which

Illus. 17. A screening box is necessary for ferreting out almandine garnets along this small stream.

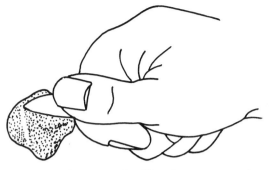

Illus. 18. Scratch your pebbles
with a penknife blade to
determine their hardness.

is softer than steel. Check once again that it is not sandstone, shale, mudstone, schist or a man-made material. If not, put it in your "soft" bag. It will polish under the right conditions.

If your pebble is not marked by your penknife blade but you *can* scratch it with your file, you have a borderline pebble which should go into your third bag for closer study at home.

This dividing of pebbles into groups of approximately equal hardness is most important in tumble-polishing. Indeed it might be said to be the key to success. Almost all disappointing results can be traced to insufficient attention to the hardness question, so do make quite sure that you carry out the simple tests described above.

There is a scale of hardness known as Mohs' Scale which is often quoted in books on geology, mineralogy and gemology. It provides a convenient means of indicating the relative hardness of one mineral when compared to another, placing diamond at the top of the scale (10) and talc at the bottom (1). Most beach pebbles worth polishing lie somewhere in the middle of this scale, and your penknife blade (hardness $5\frac{1}{2}$) and your steel file (hardness $6\frac{1}{2}$) provide two very convenient known hardnesses to enable you to group your finds.

A Closer Look at Your Hard Pebbles

Let us assume you have collected a few pounds of pebbles in your "hard" bag and you now have them spread out on your kitchen table and ready for grinding and polishing. Before you put them into the barrel, examine each one closely. Many will probably belong to the quartz family and now is a good time to get to know this family more intimately. Half an hour spent identifying and grouping your finds now will repay great dividends in the future, for you will begin to recognize pebbles and be able to name them more readily. However, it is not essential to know any more about your pebbles at this stage than that they are harder than your steel file. If you wish to skip the next section, you may do so and your pebbles will still polish well. It is included for those who wish to improve their recognition skills.

Pebbles having *quartz* as their dominant constituent are found on almost every beach and gravel bar. As you have already demonstrated for yourself, such pebbles are extremely hard. Their differences in color and appearance are due to varying amounts of other minerals in each pebble and also to the way in which the quartz has formed.

Quartz is silica and a microcrystalline sub-variety is known as *flint*—a pebble which most readers will readily identify. You will surely have some in your collection. Pick them all out now and notice the variations possible in this humble pebble; gray, brown or black in color, often appearing translucent—yet not being so when held up to strong light. Everyone knows that two flint pebbles struck against each other will produce a spark, but it is not generally known that all quartz pebbles will do the same and often produce bigger and better sparks.

You will probably confuse *chert* with flint initially because it can look very similar and differs only slightly in composition. The lighter grays and any smoky-yellow specimens in your flints are likely to be chert. (See page 28.)

Quartzite pebbles are also very likely to be included in your collection. They consist of tiny grains of quartz bonded together and usually display a very attractive network of patterns. Unlike the sandstone you have rejected, quartzite is extremely hard. This is because the sand grains in quartzite have been subjected to great pressure and heat at some time in the past and have melted and recrystallized and are now held together in a cement of pure silica. Quartzite pebbles are opaque and color variations include white, yellow and brown, often with mineral tints of blue and purple.

Quartz breccia was formed in a similar way to quartzite but you

Illus. 19. Good polishing pebbles: (1) white quartz; (2) citrine; (3) brown jasper; (4) brown beach agate; (5) yellow and green jasper; (6) jet; (7) granite; (8) rock crystal.

Illus. 20. Poor polishing pebbles: (1) quartzite; (2) fine-grained sandstone; (3) quartz vein in quartzite; (4) sandstone; (5) garnets in mica schist.

Illus. 21. Quartz breccia. Angular fragments distinguish breccias from conglomerates, which are composed of round fragments.

should have no difficulty in identifying pebbles of breccia. They consist of angular fragments of rock bonded together in a silica cement. These angular fragments are large enough to see easily and you should rely for identification on this distinctive characteristic since color variations can be wide. The other pebble which is often confused with breccia is the *conglomerate*, but a close look at the rock fragments which make up the pebble will decide the issue. The fragments in a conglomerate will be rounded (like tiny pebbles themselves) and not angular as in breccia.

Milky quartz pebbles should not be difficult to distinguish from flint and chert because they are much lighter in color (white, creamy yellow) and often translucent or nearly so. They are more likely to be confused with *banded crystalline quartz* which can be white to light brown. Look for multi-colored patterns and bands. Milky quartz does not have them; banded crystalline quartz does.

If you have been lucky enough to find *agate* pebbles (see page 25) you will recognize them by their characteristic, and very defined, banding and their wide color range—pink, red, yellow, white, brown and blue. Your file test will have already shown that agates are very hard over their entire surface, unlike veined pebbles which are softer between the veins; you will be delighted with any you polish. Disappointment might come later when you try to decide which of the varieties of agate you have found. They are grouped according to color and banding but there is a certain overlapping of groups which can be confusing. For determined readers bent on positive identification, the main groups are:

Banded agate: bands of color which are parallel to the outer surface.

Eyed agate: bands in concentric rings.

Fortification agate: angular bands.

Onyx: straight, alternating bands of black and white.

Sardonyx: bands of white and red or brown.

If any pebbles suspected of being glass which you have picked up pass your hardness test they may be *clear quartz* (rock crystal). Test them further by striking two pieces together in darkness. They should produce an orange spark and a smell of burning. Perfect quartz crystals are six-sided with six rhombohedral faces at each end, but your chances of finding such specimens on a beach are remote. Content yourself with very small, frosted pebbles which will reveal their true beauty when tumbled.

Colored varieties of rock crystal are to be found occasionally on certain beaches. The best known varieties are:

Amethyst: transparent to semi-transparent; purple to pale pink, with
  some white banding (see pages 32 and 40).

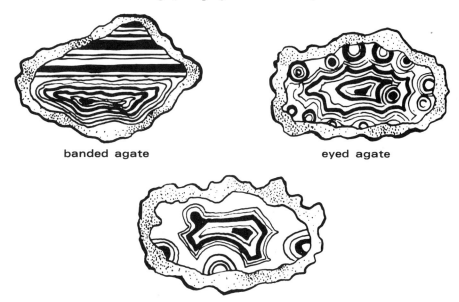

banded agate   eyed agate

fortification agate

Illus. 22. Agates are grouped according to color and banding.

27

Illus. 23. This fossilized coral called "Petoskey stone" is found on the shores of Lake Michigan.
(See page 10.)

Illus. 24. Flints and cherts occur in a variety of forms and are often difficult to tell apart.

Illus. 25. Rough pebbles. Left to right: Green quartz, serpentine, yellow quartz.

Illus. 26. The same pebbles (enlarged) after tumble-polishing.

Illus. 27. Agate hunting at Scott's Bay on Cape Blomiden, Nova Scotia. Amethysts are also available in this area.

Citrine: transparent to semi-transparent; golden yellow (see page 25).
Smoky quartz: transparent to semi-transparent; deep yellow to brown.
A variety of quartz which did not form large crystals when it cooled is known as *chalcedony.* It has a waxy luster, is translucent, and has a milky-white, blue, gray or pale brown color. It might be confused with milky quartz, but its waxiness should easily distinguish it if the two are compared when dry. The red variety, *carnelian,* is extremely beautiful when polished. These pebbles seem to glow with warm fire when held up to the light and soon catch the eye on a sunny day near the water's edge. Colors vary from pale to deep red and some impure varieties may be speckled and not wholly translucent. Sometimes iron-stained quartz pebbles are mistaken for carnelian but they lack the characteristic waxy feel and translucent warmth.

You must be very careful of the beginner's mistake of assuming that all pebbles can be neatly allocated to a particular group or variety; that each will display one set of characteristics (as set out above) which will allow you to say, "this is X, Y, or Z" with certainty. Nature did not make her pebbles for the benefit of the collector or tumble-polisher, and many of your quartz pebbles will resist all your efforts to positively identify them. Content yourself with the knowledge that they qualify as "hard" and will polish well.

The previous paragraph serves as a good introduction to four pebbles requiring special attention: jaspers, conglomerates, porphyritic pebbles and granites. All four will probably find their way into your "hard" bag at some time during your collecting expeditions and they have much in common.

You are nearly certain to have *jasper* pebbles in your "hard" bag because they are to be found on almost every beach. Jasper consists of tiny quartz grains intermingled with clay which has become colored by iron salts. Although a very ordinary pebble, it can look beautiful when polished and makes up into charming jewelry. By far the most common single-color variation is a deep red, and you should always suspect any deep red, opaque pebble of being jasper. Less common colors are yellow and green, sometimes with ribbons of clear quartz running through the pebble. Many jaspers will possess a combination of all three colors and they can be confused with conglomerates. However, jasper pebbles do not usually have the multi-coloring of conglomerates. (See page 25.)

Because it is a very common pebble, jasper is one of the first which

Illus. 28. Tumble-polished Oregon beach agates.

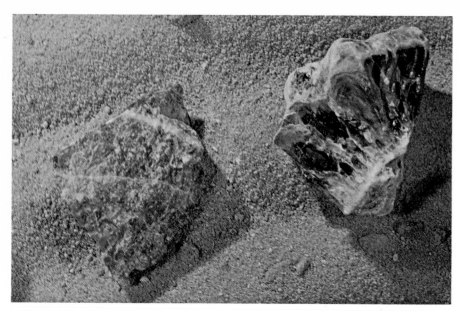

Illus. 29. Unpolished sodalite and amethyst. (See page 93 for sources.)

Illus. 30. The same pebbles as above, tumble-polished.

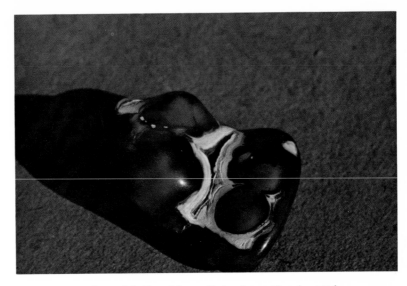

Illus. 31. Tumble-polished agatized coral.

Illus. 32. Tumble-polished Oregon beach agates.

beginners recognize readily and the temptation to drop all jasper pebbles into the "hard" bag is difficult to resist, particularly on days when you are in a hurry or the weather is unfriendly. This can lead to problems when tumble-polishing because jasper can fluctuate in hardness. If you have a high percentage of very hard quartz pebbles in the tumbling mixture, the softer jasper might break down and upset the process.

The same can be said of *conglomerates.* These pebbles are made up of rounded fragments of a variety of rocks (some of which may be quartz) cemented together in a finely textured matrix. They are usually quite beautiful and multi-colored, but fluctuations in hardness are possible.

Porphyritic pebbles are also formed from a variety of rocks but unlike conglomerates, which have rounded fragments, and quartz breccias, which have angular fragments, these pebbles consist of perfect crystals of quartz and feldspar bonded together in a hard matrix. Once again, different hardnesses are possible.

Finally *granite.* These pebbles are so widespread that you must come

Illus. 33. Quartz crystals.

Illus. 34. Left, a six-sided piece of clear quartz; middle, a similar piece sea-worn for about 10,000 years; and below, what a tumble-polisher can do in three weeks!

across them when collecting. They are composed of three minerals—quartz, feldspar and mica—and vary in color from gray to pink. The sparkle in granite is caused by particles of mica, while the pink tints are imparted to the pebble by its feldspar content. Variations in hardness are common. (See page 25.)

How then can you decide what to do with these four difficult pebbles? There are three possibilities:

1. Reject them all and stick to pure quartz—an unhappy decision because some of the most beautiful beach pebbles belong to this group.
2. Check each pebble very carefully by trying to scratch its surface in different spots—a better solution, especially if you only have a few specimens.
3. Tumble jaspers, conglomerates, porphyritic pebbles and granite together and keep the purer quartz pebbles apart—the best solution, particularly if you have a tumbler with more than one barrel.

Illus. 35. Polished blue chalcedony from Monte Lake, British Columbia.

Illus. 36. Tumbled chloramelanite, found at Big Lagoon, California.

Illus. 37. A collection of small baroques, tumble-polished and ready to mount on findings.

Illus. 38. Chalcedony after coral from Tampa Bay, Florida.

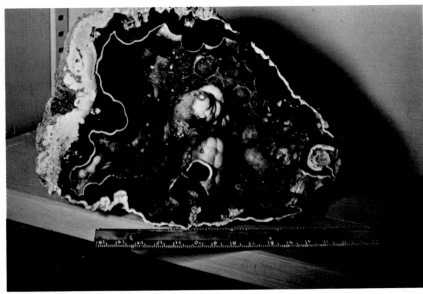

Summary of Hard Pebbles

Name	Characteristics	Sometimes confused with	Tumble with
Flint	Opaque to semi-translucent; gray, brown or black.	Chert.	Other quartz pebbles.
Chert	Opaque to semi-translucent; light gray to smoky-yellow.	Flint, limestone.	Other quartz pebbles.
Quartzite	Opaque. White, yellow, brown, often with a network of patterns and tints of blue or purple. Minute quartz grains in a hard matrix.	Conglomerates of similar hardness; jasper, quartz breccia.	Other quartz pebbles.
Quartz breccia	Opaque. Wide color variations. Angular rock fragments bounded together in a silica matrix.	Quartzite, conglomerates of similar hardness, jasper porphyritic pebbles, grit.	Other quartz pebbles.
Milky quartz	Translucent or semi-translucent. White to creamy yellow.	Banded crystalline quartz, limestone.	Other quartz pebbles.
Banded crystalline quartz	Opaque to semi-translucent. White to light brown with colored patterns or bands.	Milky quartz.	Other quartz pebbles.
Agate	Characterized by strong banding and wide color range.	Any veined pebble.	Other quartz pebbles.
Clear quartz	Transparent. Pure silica. Color variations: amethyst, citrine, smoky quartz.	Glass.	Other quartz pebbles.

Name	Characteristics	Sometimes confused with	Tumble with
Chalcedony	Translucent and waxy. Milky white, blue, gray, pale brown.	Milky quartz.	Other quartz pebbles.
Carnelian	Translucent and waxy. Pale to deep red.	Iron-stained quartz pebbles.	Other quartz pebbles.
Jasper	Opaque. Deep red, yellow, green, combinations of these —sometimes with ribbons of clear quartz.	Conglomerates, brick, quartzite, quartz breccia, serpentine.	Ideally with other jaspers, but can be tumbled satisfactorily with conglomerates, porphyritics, and harder granites. Very hard specimens with other quartz pebbles.
Conglomerates	Opaque and multi-colored. Consists of rounded fragments of rock cemented together.	Jasper, quartzite, quartz breccia, serpentine.	Ideally with other conglomerates, but can be tumbled with jasper, porphyritics, and harder granites. Very hard specimens with other quartz pebbles.
Porphyritic pebbles	Opaque. Crystals of quartz and feldspar bounded together in hard matrix.	Quartz breccia.	Ideally with other porphyritics, but can be tumbled with jasper, conglomerates, and harder granites. Very hard specimens with other quartz pebbles.
Granite	Opaque. Gray to pink with a sparkle caused by mica particles.		With other granites unless *very* hard and then best with softer jasper, conglomerates and porphyritics.

Illus. 39. Amethyst, a variety of rock crystal, varies from transparent to semi-transparent, pink to purple.

Illus. 40. Natural pyrite crystals from Litchfield, Connecticut.

Illus. 41. Just to prove you don't have to go to the far reaches of the earth, these garnets were found during a recent subway excavation in New York City!

Illus. 42. You can easily mount your polished pebbles on silver wire which you wind around the pebbles as shown here.

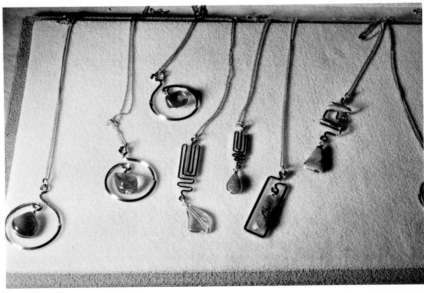

A Closer Look at Your Soft Pebbles

A few hours spent hunting pebbles on most beaches reveals that the vast majority of pebbles fall into two categories—very hard, or too soft. Nevertheless, there is a small but important category somewhere between these two extremes which includes some beautiful specimens. They are soft—but not too soft. With care they can be tumble-polished successfully and the results more than justify their special treatment.

One of the best known of the soft pebbles is *serpentine*. It is probably best identified by its feel to your fingers—a soapy, almost lubricated surface which immediately suggests softness. It is an opaque pebble and its main color variations are pale to dark green and dark red to brown, all with a mottled appearance and sometimes white veins. These might be confused with conglomerates or jasper on appearance but their feel is unique and they are, of course, much softer. (See page 29.)

The best location for serpentine pebbles is not in the United States at all but is in the Lizard area of Cornwall, England, where it can be seen in the tourists' shops. In the United States it is most everywhere—in California it is the official state rock. If you take Route 1 in California

Illus. 43. The beaches along Route 1 in California yield serpentine and jasper.

Illus. 44. Along the Fraser River in British Columbia, there are pebbles everywhere. Jade is on sale at roadside shops.

north from San Luis Obispo to Monterey you pass Jade Cove just south of Big Sur. If you take a look, watch the cliffs. The country rock here is serpentine, and when wet as it usually is from the spray or fog, it is quite slippery. The nephrite jade for which the cove is named requires a discerning eye—when wet it has a higher gloss than the serpentine. Don't make a project out of finding jade—the local collectors have picked it clean—but serpentine presents no problem. It is a leaf green, not like the red and green variety found at Cornwall, England.

Another serpentine locality is along the Fraser River in British Columbia. Try collecting near New Hope which is a tourist town about two hours northeast of Vancouver. There is even a small exhibit of local minerals in the tourist information center. Anywhere along the Fraser where the gravel bars are accessible is good pebble hunting country.

In eastern Canada, serpentine is the country rock of the asbestos

Illus. 45. There is a great variety of findings available . . .

Illus. 46. . . . for mounting your tumble-polished pebbles.

shield around Thetford Mines in the Province of Quebec. Technically, asbestos is the asbestiform variety of serpentine called *chrysotile*.

Incidentally, jade and serpentine are intertwined. Jade pebbles are mentioned as being found near San Simeon in California, a spot mentioned earlier, but they are hard to find. In northern California near Crescent City at a beach called Big Lagoon look for another variety of jade called jadeite. Here it is black streaked with green, and as a sub-variety, is called *chloramelanite* (Illus. 36). It tumbles beautifully. If you don't find any you will find black chalcedony pebbles and plenty of serpentine.

The beach at Crescent City has a good agate beach, well worth a look. It is in this stretch heading toward Oregon that you start to see rock shops featuring tumbled agate beach pebbles to whet the collecting appetite. (See Illus. 32.)

Limestone is often formed from the skeletons of plants, shells and sea urchins which lived millions of years ago and you will often find limestone pebbles which, when polished, will reveal tiny fossils of these organisms. Unfortunately, limestone varies greatly in hardness; chalk (a kind of limestone) is too soft for tumble-polishing, but some crystalline limestone can be polished in this way. Best results are probably achieved by polishing limestone pebbles from a limited area together, but the pebbles *will* polish with marble and serpentine. Limestone pebbles are opaque and can be dull white to yellow, sometimes with colorful staining. They can be confused with milky quartz and chert but are much softer than quartz and will effervesce when a weak acid such as vinegar is applied to their surface.

Marble is limestone which has been subjected to great pressure and heat. It is opaque and has a granular appearance, a crystalline sparkle and a wide color range. Although soft, it is compact and polishes well. Again, best results are achieved by loading the barrel entirely with marble, but it will polish with other soft pebbles.

Incidentally, it is worth remembering that fairly round pebbles of limestone and marble are likely to be harder (and therefore more suitable for polishing) than flattened pebbles which were easily worn by wave action.

Illus. 47. Fossils in limestone. The fossils are likely to be found as small pieces on a beach.

It is worth mentioning that *fossils* are often found when collecting beach pebbles. Indeed, some pebbles are composed entirely of fossils. Their hardness depends on the mineral which has replaced the animal or plant. If it was silica, the fossil might be seen as a pattern in hard flint or chert pebbles; if limestone, then the pebbles will be softer, though equally beautiful. Fossils could, therefore, find their way into any of your three collecting bags. At Agate Beach, Oregon, there is good collecting. (The Travel Information Div. of the Oregon State Highway Dept., Salem, Oregon puts out a pamphlet on "Minerals, Fossils, Rocks, and Where to Find Them." Don't go without it.)

Summary of Soft Pebbles

Name	Characteristics	Sometimes confused with	Tumble with
Serpentine	Opaque. Soapy, lubricated feel. Pale to dark green, and dark red to brown—all with a mottled appearance and occasionally white veining.	Conglomerates and jasper.	Ideally with other serpentine but can be tumbled successfully with limestone and marble.
Limestone	Opaque. Dull white to yellow, sometimes with colorful staining. In the harder, crystalline limestones a sparkle is characteristic. The softer limestones often reveal fossil remains. Effervesces with a weak acid.	Milky quartz, chert.	Ideally with limestone pebbles from the same area. Can be tumbled with serpentine and marble.
Marble	Limestone which has been subjected to pressure and heat. Opaque, granular, with a crystalline sparkle and wide color range.		Other marble pebbles or limestone.
Fossils	See text (page 47).		Probably better to polish by hand.

A Closer Look at What Is Left

No two pebbles are exactly alike. Frequently on New England beaches you may find the ordinary granite pebbles composed of quartz, feldspar, and granite, and then you may occasionally be puzzled by green areas in such pebbles. The green material is a mineral called epidote and the rock goes under the name of unakite. In the mountains of Virginia, North Carolina, and Tennessee, unakite is quite common and is even used for road fill. Red jasper in Vermont was used for road fill, too, but before mineral collecting became the tremendous hobby it now is.

Anything can be found on beaches. Near Westbrook, Connecticut, telltale purple-stained sands lead to almandine garnets in the adjacent low-lying mica schists. (Not quite good enough for polishing or even tumbling but interesting enough to take home.) The famous star garnets (which do tumble nicely) of Emerald Creek near St. Maries, Idaho, are another story. Collecting there requires equipment and manpower besides a trained eye and so leave that for the time when you may become a dedicated amateur mineralogist. However, the area is open and the collecting spot is near the road so you can take the family to see what is going on. There is a carnelian brook near Sterling, New Jersey, which falls into the same category as Emerald Creek. Also a carnelian location at Clear Creek, outside of Portland, Oregon. You need long shovels, $\frac{1}{4}$-inch mesh sieves, and a strong back.

Anywhere you see a sand and gravel pit, drive in. Most superintendents will be amused at the idea that gravels are a source of jewelry. In states like Alabama the gravel pits may be your best bet.

The possibilities are endless and the more knowledge and skill you acquire, the happier you will be. Your jewelry will show more imagination too.

3. Tumble-Polishing Machines

Although you may not yet have seen a man-made tumbling machine, you have certainly seen Nature's tumbler at work if you have stood on a beach and watched the rhythmical forces which are constantly at work near the water's edge. Waves breaking on the shoreline cascade their energies up onto the sloping sands. With each wave, fragments of rock are rolled up the beach and down again as the energy of each wave is spent, to be caught by the succeeding wave and rolled up once more in a never-ending cycle which carries them up, down and along the beach in a series of gentle arcs. Gradually, relentlessly, these rock fragments are transformed into smooth, round pebbles by the abrasive action of the countless grains of sand over which they roll. A single pebble may be many years in the making, but the sea never stops and the grains of sand are always there and slowly, certainly, each pebble is formed. A thousand years from now, those same rhythmical forces which produced it will have reduced it to sand grains.

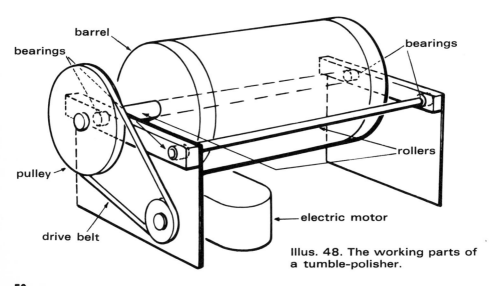

Illus. 48. The working parts of a tumble-polisher.

How They Work

It is this very same wearing-down-to-smoothness process which a tumble-polishing machine is designed to reproduce and speed up. Instead of the irresistible force of breaking waves, its energy derives from a small electric motor which turns rollers on which a barrel containing pebbles is placed. Inside the barrel, silicon carbide grits take the place of sands on the beach. As the barrel revolves, these grits wear down the roughened surfaces on each pebble to perfect smoothness. That which Nature takes years to achieve with waves and sand, the tumbling machine can produce in a matter of days. And unlike the sand on a beach, the grits in the tumbler can be carefully graded from very coarse to exceedingly fine. This means that the wearing-down process can be controlled and the smoothing process carried to a degree of perfection quite impossible to achieve with sand grains.

Even the gleaming beauty of a sea-washed pebble can be improved upon by the machine. Polishing agents, introduced into the barrel during the final stages of the process, impart a mirror-finish to each pebble which makes wet beach pebbles look quite dull by comparison. And unlike wet beach pebbles, which lose their shine as soon as they dry out, correctly tumble-polished pebbles retain their gleaming beauty forever.

The Right Machine

The first step on the road to perfect tumble-polishing is to acquire an efficient and reliable tumbling machine. The machines come in a wide variety of shapes and sizes; making the right choice at the outset can be tricky without some knowledge of the way in which the machine works and the job which each component in the machine must do.

A typical tumble-polisher consists of an electric motor which drives a pulley connected via a belt or some other method of drive to one of two parallel rollers. On these rollers a barrel containing the stones to be polished and a suitable abrasive or polish is made to revolve at a predetermined speed for a number days. During this period the abrasives in the barrel are changed at regular intervals, each change being to a finer abrasive, until the polishing stage is reached and the pebbles are ready for making into jewelry.

The whole process takes several days and during that time the electric motor must run continuously. A twenty-day cycle, for example, requires 480 hours non-stop running on the part of the motor. It is of the utmost importance, therefore, that the motor is reliable.

The pulley and belt which transfer the driving power from the motor to the rollers must also be designed to withstand continuous running. A barrel of stones is a heavy load and the job of turning it must be within the capabilities of these components. If other methods of transferring the power of the motor to the rollers are employed, they must be reliable and guarantee positive turning of the rollers at all times during operation.

Rollers and the bearings in which they run must also be designed and built to withstand the toughest wear. The rollers must be capable of withstanding all the friction of a continuously turning barrel of stones and must be of a material which does not allow the barrel to slip as it turns. At the same time they must not in any way prevent free rotation. Bearings are of the utmost importance whatever type or size of machine is considered. They must be tough enough to take long periods of hard work and be designed to allow free roller action. Lubrication must be a simple and straightforward job and must not require dismantling of the machine to carry out this essential maintenance.

Finally, you must consider the barrel which probably does more hard work than all the other components put together. A barrel constructed from inferior or non-hard-wearing materials will never stand up to the rigors of stone-polishing. It might just be possible to get away with second best on other components but if the barrel has the slightest defect it will certainly be revealed very quickly in use. As will be explained later, water must always be present during the tumbling process and if the barrel is not watertight trouble will soon develop. A leak will certainly impair the efficiency of the rollers if they become wet, and there is a danger of an electrical fault if any leaking water finds its way to the motor.

The lid of the barrel must also be wide enough to allow easy entry and exit of the pebbles and your hand because you will be putting pebbles in and taking them out many times during the barrel's working life. You will also be cleaning the barrel regularly so it must be designed in a way that eliminates corners and angles difficult to reach when washing out used abrasives. If even a few grains of a coarse abrasive are allowed to remain in the barrel during any subsequent stage in the polishing sequence the result will be an inferior finish to the final polish. Easy-to-clean, therefore, should be high on your list of points to look for when making your choice.

To summarize: A good tumble-polishing machine must

1. have a reliable motor;
2. have a strong pulley and drive belt, or other driving method;
3. have tough, hard-wearing rollers;
4. have efficient bearings;
5. be easy to lubricate and maintain;
6. have a strong, leakproof, easy-to-clean barrel.

In spite of the rigorous specifications outlined above, it does not follow that a good tumbler must be built like a battleship. Good design and the choice of lightweight but durable materials can greatly reduce cost, weight and wear. If a manufacturer has achieved low cost and light weight and is prepared to guarantee his machine against defects for any reasonable length of time, he is likely to be marketing a sound product.

There are many makes, types and sizes of machine on the market and the best advice before buying is to keep the above points in mind and buy from a reliable supplier. Such a supplier will *always* guarantee his machine against any of the faults outlined above and give you the benefit of his experience if you call at his premises.

Many of you will be buying your machines by mail and it is advisable to write to three or four suppliers initially asking for catalogs and price lists. The less expensive tumblers will not necessarily be the best, but you should be able to check on most of the points already mentioned by comparing catalogs. Incidentally, no one should worry greatly about ordering by mail. The vast majority of mail-order firms are very reliable and most sell on a refund-if-not-delighted basis.

BARREL SIZE: The size of the barrel or barrels on your tumbling machine predetermines a surprising number of things about the pebbles you can put into it. For a start, it determines the amount of pebbles you can polish at once. It is physically impossible to put ten pounds of pebbles into a barrel with a capacity of three pounds.

Secondly, it determines the size of pebbles you can polish in the barrel. A small barrel will not polish large pebbles.

Thirdly, it determines the amount of abrasive grits and polishing powder you need to carry out the process. A very large barrel needs more grits and polish than does a very small barrel.

Fourthly, because the barrel—whatever its size—must be filled to a predetermined level with pebbles, the amount of pebbles you must *collect* before you can start the operation has also been decided once you choose a particular size of barrel.

Illus. 49. Small tumbler with a single one-and-a-half-pound barrel.

Illus. 50. Small tumbler with a single three-pound barrel.

Advantages and Disadvantages of Different Models

Let us now look at five typical tumble-polishing machines with barrels of different sizes and consider their relative merits:

1. *A small tumbler with a single one-and-a-half-pound barrel:* This little machine will be quite inexpensive and will do a lot of work. Its barrel will hold approximately 100 pebbles ranging in size from equal to your little fingernail up to the size of the top joint of your thumb. It will be very economical on grits and polish and you should have no difficulty in finding enough pebbles to fill it during an hour's stroll along a good pebble beach.

Its disadvantages are:

(a) if you have collected both hard and soft pebbles and filled the barrel with the hard ones you will have to wait approximately three weeks before you can make a start on the soft ones;

(b) you will not be able to polish pebbles larger than the sizes mentioned above;

(c) if you have collected several pounds of pebbles, it will take many weeks to polish them all.

2. *A small tumbler with a single three-pound barrel:* Although slightly more expensive, this little machine will do twice the work of No. 1.

Illus. 51. A larger tumbler with two one-and-a-half-pound barrels.

You will be able to polish 200 or so pebbles at once and you will be able to include half a dozen slightly larger pebbles.

Its disadvantages are:

(a) once again you will have to wait three weeks between each batch of hard and soft pebbles;

(b) you will have to collect 200 pebbles before you can start the process. This is not difficult in summer when weekend trips to the beach are a regular feature of family life, but it is worth bearing in mind as winter approaches.

3. *A larger tumbler with two one-and-a-half-pound barrels:* This twin-barreled model has the advantage of a total capacity of approximately 200 pebbles, but what is more important is its ability to do two jobs at once. You can load one barrel with hard pebbles, the other with soft, and three weeks later they are all ready for making into jewelry. As will be explained in the chapter on polishing pebbles, there are certain advantages in keeping one barrel solely for use in the final polishing stage of the process. With this machine you can do that and still have your second barrel working on grinding other pebbles.

The only disadvantage worth mentioning with this machine is that you are, of course, limited on pebble size to the requirements of a one-and-a-half pound barrel.

4. *A larger tumbler with one three-pound barrel and two one-and-a-half-pound barrels:* This is a deluxe machine with the single disadvantage of being fairly expensive. However, its advantages more than justify its greater cost. Total capacity is around 400 pebbles, but if you happen to be low on supplies you don't have to wait until you can get down to the beach again. Simply use one of the small barrels as you would with No. 1 above. If you have a good stock of pebbles you can add some larger ones when using the three-pound barrel; you can keep one of the small barrels just for polishing; you can put three pounds of pebbles through the first and second grinding stages and then carefully select the best of the batch to fill one of your one and a half pounders. Indeed, a very versatile machine.

5. *A very large tumbler with a twelve-pound barrel:* This giant will polish 800 pebbles in one cycle, enough to keep the average home jewelry-maker going for many months. As the barrel must be filled with either hard or soft pebbles, you will need 1600 pebbles in stock, almost too many unless you are going in for jewelry-making on a commercial scale. It will, of course, polish much larger pebbles than any of the four previously mentioned.

Anyone contemplating starting a business in tumble-polishing stones is recommended to give large tumblers careful consideration. Similarly, their ability to polish quite large pebbles must not be overlooked. If you plan to use pebbles for projects other than jewelry-making and you need large quantities of bigger pebbles, a big barrel is likely to be your choice.

But whatever your choice—large, small, or in-between—you should avoid metal barrels unless they are adequately lined on the inside with hard-wearing rubber. Chemical reactions which produce gas can be set up in an unlined metal barrel if it is filled with pebbles, water and abrasive and made to revolve for any length of time on a machine. The gas, usually hydrogen, is produced by a reaction of the acids normally present in water and pebbles with the particles of

Summary

Tumbler capacity	Barrels	Advantages	Disadvantages
$1\frac{1}{2}$ lbs.	One, taking approximately 100 pebbles.	Inexpensive; easy to fill; very economical on grits and polish.	Can only tumble one load of hard or soft pebbles in one three-week cycle; limitation on pebble size.
3 lbs.	One, taking approximately 200 pebbles.	Will take *some* larger pebbles.	Can only tumble one load of hard or soft pebbles in one three-week cycle.
3 lbs.	Two, taking approximately 100 pebbles each.	Can polish hard and soft pebbles at the same time in separate barrels.	Limitations on pebble size.
6 lbs.	Three, one taking approximately 200 pebbles; two taking approximately 100 pebbles each.	Extremely versatile; large total capacity, but can also be used for tumbling small loads. Can grind hard and soft pebbles, and polish a third batch at the same time.	More expensive than any above.
12 lbs.	One, taking approximately 800 pebbles.	Will polish larger pebbles. Ideal for commercial use.	Difficult to fill owing to large capacity; can only tumble one load of hard or soft pebbles in one three-week period. Expensive.

metal which are removed from the inside of the barrel by abrasion. The danger from explosions is negligible, but the possibility of the lids being forced off or seams failing under pressure is quite high in an unlined metal barrel. The mess which results from a lid coming off a barrel unexpectedly is sufficient reason for avoiding such barrels. If you *must* use metal, make absolutely sure that the lining seals off as much of the inner surface of the barrel as is possible from contact with grits, water and pebbles.

Plastic barrels are almost problem-free as far as gas is concerned. There is no reaction between acids and metal in plastic barrels and the small amount of gas which is generated by grinding pebbles in water is dissipated when the lid is removed for regular inspection of the pebbles during the polishing process. Some recently introduced barrels have safety valves built in to provide a suitable gas vent.

The final point about choosing a tumbler applies to all models, whatever their size or method of construction. Remember that all machines are subject to wear. There will come a time when a component needs replacing or the whole machine needs servicing. At such times it is comforting to know that your supplier can help; that he has in stock any replacement part you need. If you buy a tumbler made in Timbuktu, you will probably have to take or send it back to Timbuktu if a fault develops. If, on the other hand, the manufacturer can be reached quickly by letter or telephone you will have few problems when the need for servicing arises.

The next generation of tumble-polishers are likely to have many new design features to make the job of achieving a perfect polish much easier. Already mentioned are other methods of driving the rollers, and barrels with gas vents. Other new ideas include variable speed drives which can make the rather difficult job of achieving a good polish on softer pebbles much simpler. The barrel can be slowed down during critical periods such as polishing and the final result can be carefully controlled. No doubt, these new machines will cost a little more than conventional tumblers; but for readers seeking easier methods of achieving perfection, they are worth considering.

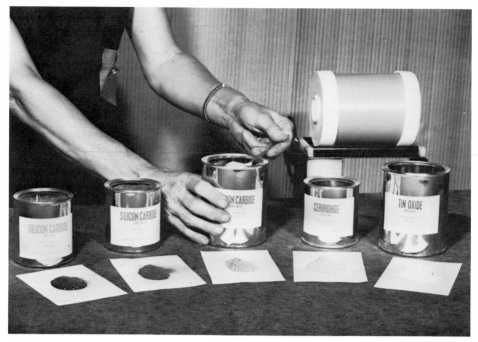

Illus. 52. Grinding and polishing compounds, ranging from very coarse (left) to finest (right).

4. Perfect Polishing

You have now arrived at the exciting moment when you start to polish. You have collected several pounds of pretty pebbles; perhaps even learned the names of and begun to recognize the more interesting ones; and you have bought yourself a tumbler and a supply of grits and polish. You are ready to start.

The first important question to settle is where you are going to keep your machine. It makes a certain amount of noise so don't choose a bedroom unless you are a heavy sleeper. Take a handful of pebbles and pour them from one hand to the other half a dozen times. That should give you some idea of the noise you will get from the machine when you start tumbling.

Next, you should consider where you least mind a bit of mess. Remember you will be filling and emptying the barrels with pebbles, water, grits, and polish many times during the machine's life.

Finally, has the spot you have selected a nearby electrical outlet where you can safely plug in your machine? You do not want yards of cord lying around for other members of the family to trip over. You should find a place at about table-top height where you can get at the machine comfortably to change grits, inspect barrels, oil bearings, and generally fuss over the thing without getting in anyone's way.

Most tumblers are probably set to work in a quiet corner of the kitchen or basement, and if you can find such a spot it should prove ideal. Spread out a dozen sheets of newspaper and stand your tumbler on them. A sheet at a time can be removed during cleaning-up operations and they will also help reduce noise by cushioning vibrations when the barrel is turning. You can fit a three-pin plug at this stage. Make quite sure you wire it correctly and make the ground connection. Tumblers are perfectly safe to run from the household electricity supply but remember you are using water in the process. To disregard safety measures which the manufacturer has built into the machine would be very foolish.

For the purpose of writing this chapter it is assumed that you have bought a tumbler similar to the six-pound model with one three-pound and two one-and-a-half pound barrels described in the previous chapter. If you have bought a different model you will find that the basic polishing process is the same with all machines and notes have been added where necessary to guide owners of smaller or larger machines. The one described has the advantage of versatility and incorporates both small and fairly large barrels so much of what follows will apply to everyone.

Grits and Polishes

We will have a closer look at these. Silicon carbide is a man-made abrasive substance which is extremely hard. You will remember the reference to Mohs' Scale in the chapter on selecting pebbles (see page 23). Silicon carbide has a hardness of more than 9.5 on that scale and is many, many times harder than the toughest pebble in your "hard" bag. It also has the advantage of forming, when made, into wedge-shaped grains, which makes it an excellent grinding material.

When manufactured by heating and then crushing a mixture of silica sand, carbon, salt and sawdust, it is then graded by being passed through a series of fine mesh screens. The familiar No. 80 grit with which almost all tumble-polishing starts gets its name from the fact that it has passed through a screen with 80 meshes to the inch.

You may have bought two or three grades of silicon carbide, depending on the manufacturer's instructions. The point to bear in mind is that the coarse grit has the *lowest* number and the finer the grit, the higher its grade number. A quick examination of the particles in each container will soon resolve matters if you are in any doubt about which is coarse and which is fine. Some manufacturers recommend mixed grades which gradually break down inside the barrel and these are excellent if the manufacturer's instructions are followed.

The two most common polishes are cerium oxide and tin oxide and you should use whichever the manufacturer recommends. *These are not grinding materials.* Their purpose is to add a permanent polish to the perfectly smooth pebbles you have produced in the earlier stages. No amount of polishing will remove any roughness you allow to remain on your pebbles after grinding. If there *is* roughness, you have not ground your pebbles long enough and you will merely waste polish if you do not put matters right by going back to an earlier grinding stage.

Last-Minute Checks

Your tumbler should have reached you in perfect condition, but you should check carefully before you switch on, especially if it reached you by mail. Check that it has been oiled and that the rollers are parallel and there are no obvious signs that the machine has received a severe blow in transit. There should be no loose wires hanging about and the belt should sit squarely in the grooves on the pulleys. If all seems well, plug in and switch on. The drive roller will turn much faster without a load and you should allow the machine to run for a few minutes like this. All moving parts should turn smoothly. If you hear odd scraping noises or if the rollers turn intermittently, something is not as it should be. Switch off at once and check your plug wiring and the manufacturer's instructions. If the machine does run smoothly, we will have a closer look at the barrels.

Loading Your Barrels

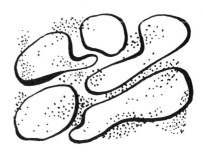

Illus. 53. A variety of shapes and sizes is the key to success when selecting pebbles for the tumbler. The small stones grind into the hollows of the larger ones.

Take the lid off one of your barrels and look inside. The inner walls should be perfectly smooth. If your barrels are metal and have rubber linings, make sure that the lining is correctly fitted and there are no bulges or loose seams. If the lid is fitted with a gasket or rubber seal, this too should be correctly seated.

You will have already sorted your pebbles into hard and soft groups, so let us start with your hard ones. Go through them once again to seek out any that have slipped through into the wrong bag. Now is the time to discard badly cracked specimens. The first grind is a tough operation and any cracked specimens are unlikely to survive. For a one-and-a-half pound barrel you will need approximately one hundred pebbles, the largest not more than one inch across; the smallest approximately a quarter of an inch. Try to select a range of shapes—ovals, spheres, discs—because the grinding action is more efficient when different shapes are mixed together.

A three-pound barrel will require approximately two hundred pebbles and you will be able to include half a dozen larger specimens— up to a maximum size of two inches. Similarly, larger barrels will take

Illus. 54. Here is a good variety of pebbles, both in size and shape.

more pebbles with a proportionate number of big ones. All, however, require a grading of sizes from large to small, with plenty of variety in shape.

Note that this section is entitled, "Loading Your Barrels"—*not* filling them. Tumbler barrels must never be filled as cans of beans are filled. If they are, they will never polish pebbles. The tumbling action depends on there being sufficient space inside the barrel to allow the pebbles to fall, one over the next, as the barrel revolves.

Too much space and too few pebbles is just as bad as overfilling. If you do not put sufficient pebbles into the barrel, they do not ride up the walls to the point where tumbling commences. They slide back to the bottom and all you get out of the barrel are badly polished, flattened discs. So do make a point of getting the amount right. A little under three-quarters full of pebbles of different shapes and sizes should be your aim. This applies to any size of barrel. Place the pebbles inside gently. You spent a long time selecting perfect specimens and it would be a pity to crack or scratch them now. Shake the barrel gently to settle them as you put them in and stop when you near the three-quarters-full point.

Many books and articles emphasize that tumbling is a mechanical process and that the operator has no control over the finished results. This is not true. *You* are in control of the operation from start to finish. You select the pebbles; you decide when they are ready for the next stage; you polish them. You may not see the entire operation, but how well you conduct and control the process determines the quality of the polish you achieve. You should keep this in mind as you proceed. Learn by observation and trial and error the best ways of doing each operation. No book can tell you when a particular batch of pebbles is ready for the next stage. You must learn to judge this by experience, learning all you can from your early mistakes and aiming with each new batch of pebbles to improve on your previous results.

There are two excellent ways in which you can start on this road to success now. The first is to keep back a small selection from each batch of pebbles you put into the barrel. Half a dozen will do. Make sure they are representative of the ones you do polish in collecting location, type, color and size. Put them into a small box or bag and

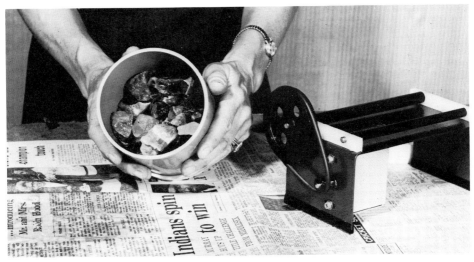

Illus. 55. This is a proper load for a barrel—approximately three-quarters full. Overloading and underloading both result in failure.

label it so that you know from which location you collected them. If you have come across any pebbles you were unable to identify from that particular spot and you wish to know how they will polish, you have only to wait and see. This type of comparison—unpolished pebble with finished result—is worth a hundred color illustrations in any book, and you will soon be able to recognize those pebbles from a particular location which polish well. Incidentally if you have more than one barrel and they look alike, stick a strip of adhesive tape or plaster on each lid and number your barrels *a, b, c,* etc. This will avoid confusion later.

The second helpful suggestion is to keep a simple progress chart so that you can record the dates and times you commence and finish different stages in the process, together with comments on results achieved. This information will prove invaluable when next you polish a batch of similar pebbles and you wish to try variations in grinding and polishing times in an effort to better your previous results. Keeping such records and retaining a few pebbles from each batch for comparisons will very soon lead you to perfection in polishing.

You can work out a log similar to the one below for any make or type of tumbler. Read the manufacturer's instructions first—particularly with regard to the number of stages in progress—and prepare your chart accordingly. A school exercise book suitably ruled makes an excellent log. Hang it up somewhere near the machine and get into the habit of keeping entries up to date. It will prove to be a mine of information during the months ahead.

A Grinding and Polishing Chart

Description of pebbles. Types, where collected	Barrel number	Days on coarse grind	Days on medium grind	Days on fine grind	Days on polish	Hours on final wash	Results and comments
EXAMPLE: Agates from Tillamook, Oregon	1	5	4	4	4 Polycel added	6	Good polish Might have been improved by longer medium/ fine stages

Illus. 56. Add the amount of coarse silicon carbide recommended by the manufacturer for your barrel size.

The First Grind

Now that you have loaded your barrel with pebbles you must add the coarse silicon carbide. The amount of grit depends on the barrel's capacity. A one-and-a-half-pound barrel requires a heaped table-spoonful, while a three-pound barrel requires twice that amount. Check the manufacturer's instructions for other barrel sizes and act accordingly. You should never put too much or too little grit into the barrel as this will upset the grinding process. Use a clean, dry spoon to measure the amount required and shake it evenly over the pebbles in the barrel.

It is of the utmost importance that you do not contaminate the grits and polish, especially by getting any of the coarse grit into the finer material or polish. Keep them well apart. If you can find a few old metal cookie or tea canisters or similar containers, they make excellent holders for your materials. Label the tins and keep them out of harm's way.

Illus. 57. Add just enough water to cover the pebbles. Do it slowly so you will not have to pour off any excess or you will reduce the quantity of grit as well.

The next step is to run tap water into the barrel until it just covers the top of the pebbles. Don't *fill* the barrel with water. Stop as soon as you see the water cover the pebbles and put the lid on the barrel. You must replace the lid so that it forms a watertight fit on the barrel. Some lids will screw on; others will be a push fit; and some will be fixed by nuts and bolts. All can be prevented from fitting correctly if grains of grit are allowed to remain on the lid or the part of the barrel which comes into contact with the lid. Wipe this area carefully before putting the lid in place and read the manufacturer's instructions for achieving a watertight fit before putting the barrel on the rollers. When you have the lid on, wipe the outside of the barrel to remove water and grit and check that water is not leaking around the cap. If all is well, switch on the tumbler and place the barrel onto the turning rollers. The rollers will immediately slow down under the weight of the barrel but should settle down at once to a steady speed of revolution. Watch the barrel for a minute or two, checking for a steady rotation and no water leaks.

Although you cannot see inside the barrel as it turns on the rollers, you can tell a great deal about what is happening inside by listening to the sound of the pebbles as they grind. The pebbles should be tumbling or rolling one over the next as they near the top of the barrel in a continuous, rhythmical motion. If you have proceeded this far and followed all the advice given above, that is the gentle, rolling sound you should hear. If you hear bangs and knocks, or the sound of pebbles falling and hitting each other, something is wrong. You have not put sufficient pebbles into the barrel, or you have put too many of the wrong size. If you hear little or no movement you have put too many pebbles into the barrel and the tumbling action is not operating.

You are about to discover that tumble-polishing requires a good deal of patience because now you must allow the barrel to turn on the rollers for the next twenty-four hours without interruption. This is always difficult for beginners who find it hard to resist taking the barrel off the rollers every hour or so to see what has happened to their precious pebbles. Very little happens in one hour. But slowly, gradually, your pebbles are being worn to smoothness. When twenty-four hours has passed you can take the barrel off and carefully open the lid. You will probably find it easier to switch off the motor when removing the barrel during the first few days, but you should soon get the knack of lifting the barrel cleanly and neatly from the rollers without stopping the machine—and replacing it just as expertly when you have finished your inspection.

Once the lid is off, you should see a dark gray liquid (slurry). Working over a sink, with the tap turned on, carefully lift out half a dozen pebbles. Shake off as much of the slurry as possible before moving them clear of the barrel. Put the barrel to one side and run the pebbles you have removed under the tap to wash away all traces of the gray liquid. Now examine the washed pebbles carefully. Already they will feel smoother to your fingers, but they have a long way to go to perfection. Select one of the pebbles and dry it carefully. Now examine it under a good light and you will see the tiny pits and cracks on its surface.

Back into the barrel it must go, along with the others you removed. Wash the lid and the top of the barrel to remove all traces of grit and replace the lid as you did before. Once you are satisfied that you have a watertight seal, switch on the tumbler and replace the barrel on the rollers. Again, watch it for a minute or two to check for leaks. If all is well, wait another day and repeat the inspection.

You alone must decide when your pebbles are ready for the next stage. Fairly smooth beach pebbles composed mainly of quartz will take between three and six days to grind to the required smoothness. The aim is to remove all surface blemishes, pits and cracks from every pebble in the barrel, but this perfection is rarely, if ever, achieved. If you continue coarse grinding until the worst pebble in the barrel is perfectly smooth, the remainder will be too much reduced in size. Indeed, the smallest could be ground away completely if you allowed the first stage to go on too long. A compromise is what your aim should be.

When the day comes that four, or possibly five, of the half-dozen pebbles you remove for inspection satisfy you by their smoothness and blemish-free appearance that they are ready, it is time to call a halt. Remove all the pebbles from the barrel and place them in the sink with the tap running. A wire strainer or colander makes an excellent container for the pebbles at this stage. Let the tap run onto them to wash away all traces of grit.

You must not under any circumstances pour the sludge in the barrel down the waste pipe. It will very quickly block your drains and you will be faced with an expensive plumbing job. The best way to dispose of it is to find a suitably sized plastic bag and carry it, with the barrel, to the garbage can. Pour the contents of the barrel into the bag and put the bag into the garbage can.

Now, back to the kitchen and wash everything—pebbles, barrel, lid, your hands, and then wash the pebbles again. If you have made a mess around the machine, remove one of the sheets of newspaper after cleaning the rollers on the tumbler. Now is probably a good time to lubricate the roller bearings and carry out any other weekly maintenance recommended by the manufacturer. Do this before you remove a sheet of newspaper and you will be shipshape for the next stage in the process.

Illus. 58. At the end of the first stage, the pebbles should be perfectly smooth. Place them in a colander and wash thoroughly under running water.

Step by step through the first stage:

1. Check your tumbler.
2. Load barrel just less than three-quarters full with suitably sized pebbles.
3. Add correct amount of coarse grit.
4. Add water—just covering pebbles.
5. Clean cap and barrel.
6. Replace cap and check that it is watertight.
7. Switch on tumbler and place barrel on rollers, again checking for leaks.
8. Inspect daily—remember to carry out steps 5 and 6 each time.
9. When pebbles are ready, remove them from the barrel.
10. Dispose of sludge in the garbage can.
11. Wash everything very carefully.
12. Carry out machine maintenance.

Illus. 59. Before the second grind, inspect the pebbles carefully for quality.

Quality Control

We have now arrived at a point where many beginners fall by the wayside along the path to perfect polishing. The task is simple: dry your pebbles carefully, spread them out on a sheet of newspaper, examine them and reject every one that retains a blemish, pit, or crack. Ruthlessness is what is required and many beginners lack it. They allow poor quality pebbles to slip through to the next stage instead of eliminating them at this stage. When, at the end of the process, they gaze forlornly at the final result they blame the machine, the manufacturer or their own bad luck when all the time the fault is their own. So do be ruthless. The pebbles you reject now can be put back into the barrel when you start your next coarse grind and you will probably be delighted with the result. Meanwhile, put them aside.

This rejection process will of course reduce the bulk of your pebbles by about 5 or 10 per cent. The coarse silicon carbide will also have rendered each pebble smaller in size and the combined effect of rejection and wear will probably reduce the entire batch by up to 15 per cent of its original volume.

If rejection has been high, or wear very great, and you only have one barrel on your tumbler, this can mean that you are unable to load it correctly for the next stage. This ceases to be a problem when you have been tumbling for some time. You will always have odd polished pebbles lying around which for one reason or another you have not made into jewelry, and these can be used as fillers to make up the bulk of the load. If you have a very small, single-barreled tumbler, there are two courses of action you can take if the bulk of your pebbles falls below a minimum two-thirds loading line and you have not built up a stock of polished pebbles from which to draw to make up the load.

1. Put to one side the pebbles you have already processed through the first stage and start again with a new load of pebbles. When this second load has been coarse-ground, you will have more than enough pebbles to continue to the next stage.

2. Accept that you will not achieve perfection at your first polishing attempt and continue to the second stage with all the pebbles you have put through the first stage.

If you are lucky enough to have a tumbler with large *and* small barrels and you loaded one of your large barrels to begin with, you will now begin to see the advantages of your machine. Simply load a smaller barrel from the pebbles you have left after rejecting all the cracked and pitted specimens and continue with the next stage.

The Second Grind

Whichever course you decide upon, the next steps are to check that your tumbler is working correctly, and that your barrel is absolutely clean and free from all traces of coarse grit, then load it once more to just less than three-quarters full with pebbles. Take your container of finer grit, add the correct amount to the barrel and then cover the pebbles with water again. Secure the cap, after carefully cleaning it, and place the loaded barrel onto the rollers once more.

This second stage in the tumbling process is the most important of all. It is also the stage at which many attempts at perfection fail because most beginners are apt to regard it as a grinding process similar to the first grind with coarse grit. But it is much more.

During the first two or three days the fine silicon carbide *does* in fact continue the grinding process begun by the coarse grit. Scratches and tiny imperfections—some of them made by the coarse grit—are gradually worn away. It is at this point that the real work of the second stage begins. The fine grit starts to break down. It loses its power to remove scratches and pitmarks and now prepares the pebble for the final polish. You will see now why there is little to be gained from leaving badly pitted pebbles in the barrel at the end of the first stage. So little grinding takes place during the second stage that any deep imperfections cannot be removed. What you must also see is the importance of continuing the second stage until the pebbles *are* ready for polishing. Be patient. Be prepared, if necessary, to run this stage twice as long as the coarse grind. Your final results depend on it.

Fortunately, it is quite easy to decide when the pebbles have been long enough in the barrel on this stage. You will, of course, be checking their progress daily by opening the barrel and carefully washing half a dozen pebbles under the tap before examining their surfaces. What you are looking for is absolute smoothness over the entire surface of each pebble. The smallest pitmarks will ruin the final polish, so examine your samples very, very carefully. At the end of this stage the pebbles should look exactly as they will when polished—except for their lack of shine. A matt finish probably best describes what you must aim for. When it will come depends on a number of variable factors, but you might begin to expect it five or six days after commencing your second stage.

If, on examination, you think that your samples are ready, take a small piece of felt and soak it under the tap. Next, sprinkle a small amount—half a teaspoonful would be more than enough—of your polishing powder onto the wet felt. Take one of your sample pebbles firmly between finger and thumb and rub it vigorously backwards and forwards over the impregnated felt forty or fifty times. Now, carefully dry the area of pebble you have polished and examine it very closely in good light. Look for tiny pin pricks or scratches on the polished surface. If you see even one, you must continue the second stage for at least another twenty-four hours before test-polishing another pebble. If you are quite satisfied that the surface you have polished is perfect, the second stage is complete.

Incidentally, if you do see tiny pin pricks or scratches when you examine your sample, do not under any circumstances add more fine grit to the barrel in the hope that you will speed up the process. You will do quite the reverse. After five or six days of second-stage tumbling your pebbles are nearing their final smoothness, and even fine silicon carbide will scratch them. If you add more grit now you will have to begin the second stage again. The correct procedure is to put the pebbles back into the barrel and continue until you can achieve a perfect polish on the test specimen.

Step by step through the second stage:
1. Make sure you have washed away all traces of coarse grit from pebbles, barrel, caps and rollers.
2. Load barrel just less than three-quarters full with selected pebbles from the first run. (Or continue with all pebbles if you have only one barrel and this is your first attempt at polishing.)
3. Add correct amount of fine grit.
4. Add water—just covering pebbles.
5. Clean cap and barrel top.
6. Replace cap and check that it is watertight.
7. Switch on tumbler and place barrel on rollers. Check for leaks.
8. Inspect daily—remember to carry out steps 5 and 6 each time.
9. After five or six days, test-polish one pebble on a piece of felt impregnated with polishing powder.
10. If satisfactory, remove pebbles carefully from barrel.
11. Dispose of sludge in garbage can.
12. Wash everything very carefully. Take even more care than you did after the first grind.
13. Carry out machine maintenance.

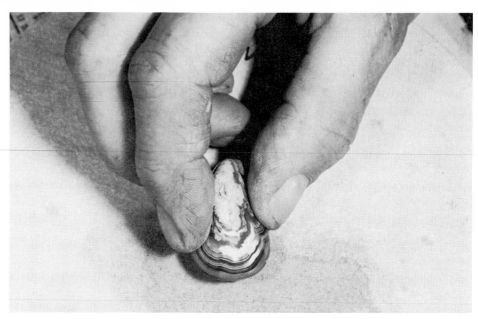

Illus. 60. After a few days on the second grind, test-polish one pebble on a piece of felt impregnated with polishing compound.

The Final Polish

You now have a batch of unpolished but perfectly smooth pebbles and your aim should be to impart a mirror-finish to each one. Handle them very carefully at this stage. Don't pour them from one container to another. When washing them to remove every trace of silicon carbide, don't allow them to knock one against the other. The smallest scratch or chip will show up when they are polished, so do handle with care.

Owners of versatile, multi-barreled tumblers will be able to keep one barrel solely for final polishing without additional expense and, although it means further outlay on equipment, buying a second barrel for this purpose is recommended to owners of single-barreled machines. If your aim is perfection in polishing, a second barrel is a worthwhile investment because it reduces to nil the chances of odd particles of silicon carbide remaining in the barrel after the second stage has been completed. Very careful washing of the inside of the barrel will do much to prevent this if you must limit expense, but remember that tiny scratches on the barrel's inner surface can trap grit particles which will resist your efforts to remove them with water.

Having made sure that the barrel you are going to use is absolutely clean, place the pebbles carefully inside, one at a time, until you have the required load—that is, just under three-quarters full. There will have been little reduction in volume during the second stage because, as already explained, so little grinding takes place. If you had the correct load at the beginning of the second stage you should have just the right amount now.

Take your container of polishing powder and add the correct amount of polish to the barrel. Cover the pebbles with clean water, replace the cap, make sure that everything is clinically clean, and return the barrel to the rollers.

As already pointed out, sound plays an important part in tumble-polishing. During this final stage you should pay particular attention to the sound of your pebbles as they tumble in the barrel. A steady and rhythmical motion inside the barrel will produce the steady and rhythmical sound of pebbles tumbling one over the next. Any harsh banging or unrhythmical striking of pebbles together is a sure sign that the tumbling action is not being carried out. If this is allowed to happen during the polishing stage, it will certainly produce cracks and scratches on the pebbles' surfaces.

The commonest cause of cracks and scratches at this stage is an insufficient load. With too few pebbles in the barrel the load is thrown about violently, causing one pebble to strike against the next so harshly that cracks and scratches are the inevitable result. This should not happen if you have followed all the advice given so far, but if you do hear any irregular sounds during the first twenty-four hours of the polishing stage, you should remedy the situation at once.

Remove the barrel from the rollers, take off the lid, and add a small amount of wallpaper paste to the mixture. The aim is to thicken the liquid in the barrel so that it cushions the fall of each pebble. Do not make the mixture too thick, otherwise the effectiveness of the polishing agent could be reduced. A thin-cream consistency is ideal and it is better to err on the side of thinness rather than add too much at the outset. The addition of the paste will, you may notice, reduce the noise your pebbles make as they tumble. It also increases the time you must allow for the polish to do its work because movement inside the barrel is reduced owing to the greater viscosity of the thickened liquid. A polishing stage of four days without paste might take seven days if paste is added.

The noise reduction question is often in the minds of beginners— especially if they live in apartments or cannot find an out-of-the-way spot for their machine. The noise is not very considerable and you should never disregard safety or the final results you wish to achieve when considering noise reduction. Do not put your machine into a padded box. The motor will overheat if adequate ventilation is not provided. Pads of rubber or felt under the base of the machine will do almost as much in the way of reducing noise and they will not prevent ventilation. You should regard the noise reduction achieved by the addition of wallpaper paste at the polishing stage as incidental. The paste is put in to prevent cracking and scratching of the pebbles. Do not, by the way, add paste during the earlier grinding stages in an effort to reduce noise—unless you are prepared to accept very long first and second stages.

Daily inspection of your pebbles is just as important at the polishing stage as it is during grinding so do not neglect it. The process should take from four to seven days to complete and only experience will tell you when the polish has done its work. There comes a time in the process when no amount of further polishing will improve the finish. Indeed, if the barrel were allowed to turn for an excessively long period, the final polish would deteriorate. Daily inspection, your log book, and experience will guide you on this point. If you examine half a dozen pebbles each day and stop the process on the day you see no improvement on the previous day's polish, your results should be satisfactory.

Step by step through the final polish:

1. Double-check that all traces of silicon carbide have been removed from your pebbles by thoroughly washing them in running water.
2. Place your pebbles very carefully into the polishing barrel. (If you are using the same barrel it *must* be clinically clean.)
3. Add correct amount of polishing powder.
4. Add water—just covering pebbles.
5. Replace cap and check that all is watertight.
6. Switch on the tumbler and place barrel on rollers, again checking for leaks.
7. If tumbling action sounds harsh, add a small amount of wallpaper paste to the barrel.
8. Inspect daily. Remember to carry out step 5 each time.
9. When polish cannot be improved upon, carefully remove pebbles from barrel.
10. Dispose of sludge in garbage can.
11. Wash everything very carefully.
12. Carry out machine maintenance.

The Last Wash

The polishing powder leaves a film on the pebbles which is removed by placing the pebbles in the cleaned barrel, covering with water, and adding not more than half a teaspoonful of detergent to break down the surface tension of the water. Run the barrel for four to eight hours, then remove the pebbles very carefully and wash off the detergent in running water. Place all the pebbles on a soft cloth and allow them to dry.

If you keep a careful log of all your tumbling for three or four months you should certainly be able to achieve perfection at the end of that time. Experiment with longer or shorter runs, different amounts of grit and polish, and pebbles of different hardnesses. This is the best way to serve your apprenticeship in tumbling and it will soon make you a master or mistress of the art. Nothing should go very wrong if you follow each step, each process, logically. If it does, reference to past experience should soon put matters right.

Fault Finding

For quick guidance, following is a list of common faults and sug-gested causes:

Fault	Possible cause
Machine runs intermittently, or stops	Badly wired plug; lubrication of bearings not carried out; oil on drive belt or rollers.
Pebbles still rough after first and second grind	Overloaded barrel; insufficient grit; barrel slipping on rollers; hard and soft pebbles mixed.
Pebbles badly cracked after first grind	Underloaded barrel; poor specimens.
Inferior polish achieved	Second stage grind not long enough; insufficient polish; hard and soft pebbles mixed in barrel.
Flats develop on pebbles	Underloaded barrel; speed of revolution too slow.
Leaking barrel	Caps not fitted correctly; grit particles not removed from cap or barrel.

5. Jewelry-Making

Let's make one point absolutely clear at the very outset: jewelry made with tumble-polished pebbles is not imitation jewelry. Each piece you make—ring, pendant, brooch or bracelet—is exclusively yours. No two pebbles are exactly alike and nobody else will ever make or own jewelry exactly the same. Select your pebbles carefully, choose your findings wisely, make the piece to the best of your ability, and the end product will be an object of beauty and originality which will give pleasure forever.

Baroque jewelry, as all jewelry made from tumble-polished pebbles is known, is extremely simple to create. Essentially it involves nothing more than glueing pebbles to findings and perhaps bending a few pieces of wire; yet at the same time it allows you to use your artistic flair to decide the color, size, shape, balance and final appearance of every piece you make. All of the art which goes into the making of costly pieces in diamond, emerald or pearl can be found in the best pieces of baroque jewelry and the fact that you found your "gems" on a beach or along a mountain stream should in no way lower your artistic aims.

Basic Equipment

You have just spent several weeks producing perfectly polished pebbles, so don't begrudge a little time spent getting together the other basic materials of the craft. There are not many, so let us go through them carefully:

A pair of short, thin-nosed pliers are all you should ever need for bending or straightening wire and they are a worthwhile buy for two reasons. They will save time and will do a neater job than fingers alone could ever do. If you are lucky, you might find an old pair in a tool box or garage, but if you have to buy, they should cost only a few dollars.

A silicon carbide abrasive stick is nothing more than a solid piece of the

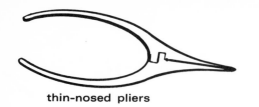
thin-nosed pliers

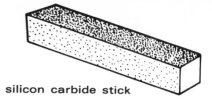
silicon carbide stick

Illus. 61.

very abrasive you have used already to grind your pebbles to smoothness. In stick form it is ideal for roughening up findings and stones prior to glueing. It costs very little.

A wooden fixture will provide you with a very useful second pair of hands to hold chains and bracelets when attaching mounted stones. It can be made by anyone capable of using a hammer and nails. Use three pieces of $2'' \times 1''$ softwood, all 9 inches long. Hammer two, $1\frac{1}{2}''$, narrow-headed nails about halfway into the narrower side of one of your pieces of wood. The first nail should be fixed 2 inches from the end of the block; the second near the middle. Next, do exactly the same to your second piece of wood. Now nail your third piece across the top of the two pieces you have hammered nails into, making sure

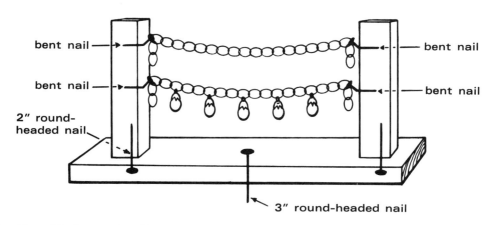

bent nail — bent nail

bent nail — bent nail

2" round-headed nail

3" round-headed nail

Illus. 62. A wooden fixture you can make yourself is a handy aid for holding findings during mounting.

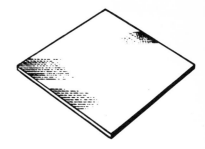

Illus. 63. A broiler pan (left) filled with sand is ideal for holding pebbles during mounting. Use a piece of glass (right) for preparing adhesives.

that the protruding nails point inward toward each other. Now turn the whole thing upside-down, bend the protruding nails upward to an angle by tapping them with your hammer, and your fixture is made. If you are lucky enough to have a workbench you can nail the fixture to the bench for extra support.

Item four on your list should be very easy to get hold of. This is an *old broiler pan* or *shallow roasting pan*. The lid of a cookie tin would serve almost as well, though it is rather shallow and the broiler pan's handle (if it has one) will be found most useful. The container is filled with sand and its purpose is to hold pebbles while findings are being glued to them. The pebbles are pressed firmly into the sand, thus leaving both hands free for placing the glued findings in position. As the adhesive used takes some time to set, the sand tray ensures a safe place for the pebbles during the hardening period and leaves you free to continue with other tasks.

A small piece of glass or *plastic-laminated board* is useful as a mixing palette when preparing the adhesive. Both can be easily cleaned after use and, their surfaces being non-absorbent, there is no danger of contaminating the adhesive.

The adhesive is an epoxy resin. It is an all-purpose adhesive and you are quite likely to have some already either in the garage or your tool box. If not, a box should cost very little and you will have enough to make many hundreds of jewelry items. The box contains two tubes—

Illus. 64. Use epoxy resin and hardener for attaching your pebbles to the findings.

one the resin, the other the hardener. Before use, correct quantities from each tube must be thoroughly mixed together on a clean, dry, non-absorbent surface—the glass or plastic-laminated board—and the resultant mixture must be used within a very short time. Unlike ordinary glue, epoxy resin sets and hardens by a chemical process which cannot be stopped once the hardener and resin have been mixed. For this reason only very small quantities, ideally the exact amount you need to make a particular batch of jewelry items, should be mixed at any one time.

For applying the epoxy resin to the findings before glueing, you will find different-sized *darning needles* to be ideal. Push the points into small corks and use the eye ends to pick up the small quantities of adhesive used to glue each piece.

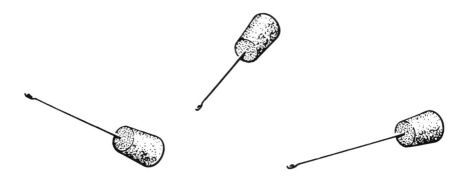

Illus. 65. Darning needles stuck into corks are useful for applying adhesive.

Illus. 66. Bell caps.

Findings

Finally, we come to the jewelry findings themselves. (See Illus. 45.) There are hundreds for you to choose from—rings, bracelets, chains, ear wires, ear screws, brooches, cuff links, tie bars, tie tacks, key rings, necklaces—all in a wide variety of styles and finishes. They can be purchased in a selection of metals—sterling silver, gold, silver-plated, gold-plated, stainless steel, or simply gold and silver colored alloy— and your choice depends on what you wish to pay. But whatever metal or style of finding you select, there are only two basic ways in which your pebbles are attached to the mountings. They are the *bell-cap* method or the *pad* method.

A bell cap is used to make pendants, necklaces, bracelets and earrings. It consists, as its name suggests, of a hollow, bell-shaped body surmounted by a tiny ring and it is secured, cap-like, onto the pebble. The bell-shaped body is made up of flexible, petal-like prongs of metal which are very easy to bend.

They can be molded with the fingers to fit snugly over the end of any pebble where they are secured with epoxy resin. The bell-capped pebble can then be fixed to a chain, bracelet, or ear wire by means of a *jump ring*. This is a small circle of springy metal which can be opened,

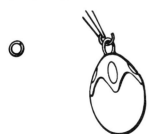

Illus. 67. Attaching a jump ring.

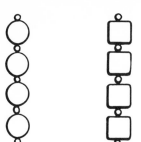

Illus. 68. Pad-type findings are ideal for rings, brooches, and cuff links.

using a pair of thin-nosed pliers, to allow the ring at the top of the bell cap and a link from a piece of chain or a bracelet to be coupled together.

Both bell caps and jump rings come in several sizes. The smallest bell caps are no longer than match heads while the largest can be $\frac{1}{2}$ inch long. Jump rings to suit each size available and the size required depends on the size of the pebble, the aim always being to use the smallest possible bell cap and jump ring for the piece being made.

The *pad* method of fixing is used to make rings, brooches, cuff links and other items in which the pebble is attached directly to the finding and not hung onto it by means of a bell cap. Once again sizes differ, particularly in rings and bracelets, and the choice of finding is determined by the size of pebble you wish to use for the job.

Making Your Jewelry

Let us now go step by step through the work involved in making some pieces of jewelry using both methods of fixing. First find yourself a clear working area and lay out your equipment as follows:

Pebbles. Select the very best of your round and pear-shaped pebbles for bell-capping and set aside any with a flat side for pad mounting.

Sand tray. Prepare this (salt can be used if sand is not readily available) by filling to a depth of 2 inches and shaking until level. Press your pebbles into the sand to about half their depth, making sure that the more pointed ends are upward. Space them evenly across the tray.

Bell caps. Take various sizes, spread the prongs and sit one on top of each pebble. Mold the prongs to the contours of the pebble. Experiment with different sizes and types to achieve the best possible artistic effect. Bear in mind that the position of the eye on the top of the cap determines how the pebble will hang from the jump ring. If you want a particular side of a pebble to face "forward" you must position your bell cap accordingly.

Do not touch the tops of the pebbles with your fingers at this stage. Hold them around their middles. The oil in your skin can prevent a good bond when you cement the bell caps in position.

Epoxy resin. Do not start to mix this until you are quite satisfied that all bell caps selected are suitable. Then, having read the instructions carefully, squeeze the correct amount of resin and hardener onto your glass plate and mix very thoroughly.

Needles. Take a corked needle and pick up a small amount of mixed adhesive on the "eye" end. Lift up your first bell cap and carefully place a blob of adhesive inside the cap. Replace the cap on the pebble and press down firmly. At this stage the adhesive is *not* holding the cap in position. The cap is balanced on top of the pebble and it is important that it remains balanced for the next hour, so do not set it at an odd angle on the pebble.

Continue to lift and replace each pebble with its blob of adhesive until you have worked your way through the tray.

Leaving your tray on the workbench, light the broiler of your stove and turn it as high as possible. Let it burn for a few minutes, then carefully carry your tray of bell-capped pebbles from the bench and place it under the burning broiler. Watch the prongs of the bell caps very carefully at this stage. After thirty seconds or so you will see the adhesive begin to flow from underneath the bell cap. The moment this happens pull out the tray. This must be done quickly, but gently. If the tray is knocked, all the bell caps will fall off.

Place the tray on a level surface away from heat and do not touch it for the next hour. When one hour has passed, every bell cap will be firmly cemented to its pebble and the adhesive will have dried clear, colorless and almost unnoticeable.

If working with children or in a spot where access to a hot broiler is impossible, the tray of pebbles can be left to bond without heat quite successfully. Proceed as above until every bell cap has been replaced

Illus. 69. Attaching a polished pebble to a bell-cap finding to make a pendant. Notice the steel spring clip on the right which is handy for holding the pebble and cap in position until the adhesive hardens.

with its blob of adhesive on its pebble and leave the tray undisturbed for twenty-four hours. An equally good bond should be the result.

In the "broiling" method, it is most important that the adhesive is not "overcooked." Remove the tray from under the heat the moment you see the epoxy begin to run. If this is not done, it will discolor on hardening to an unpleasant brown.

The fixture. When glueing is completed, you can proceed to make necklaces, pendants and bracelets. Hook pieces of chain or bracelet onto the bent nails of your fixture; work out the correct spacing of each pebble; and slip jump rings through the links on the chain or bracelet where required with the aid of your pliers. Select bell-capped pebbles according to shape, size and color, and, using your pliers once again, couple them to your chain or bracelet by means of the jump rings.

Although slightly different methods are used for pad findings, the aim remains the same: a perfect bond between finding and pebble. This is best achieved by roughening the two surfaces to be joined with your *silicon carbide stick*. A few scratches on the pad and two or three strokes of the stick across the pebbles are all that is required.

Rings should be scratched in this way and then set in the sand tray in the same way as the pebbles were set for bell-capping. Scratch the area of the pebbles you wish to join to the ring pad *before* you mix your adhesive and proceed as for bell-capping. If using the quicker "broiler" method for bonding, you will find that the epoxy takes a few seconds longer to flow because it is protected from the heat by the pebble. How much longer depends on the size of the pebble because a larger pebble shields the resin from the heat far more than does a small pebble. It is probably better, therefore, to make rings with similar-sized stones in one batch.

Cuff links and ear screws should be dealt with in the same way as rings. Set the finding in the sand tray after scratching the pad with the abrasive stick and glue the pebble to the finding.

Bracelets should be laid out on the sand after each pad has been scratched. Pebbles of different sizes, shapes, and colors can then be tried on the pads before they are scratched and cemented. Again, it is probably better to work with pebbles of similar sizes.

There are so many different types of *brooches* available that the choice of whether to place the finding or the pebble in the sand tray must be left to you. If you can balance the brooch on top of the pebble without fear of it slipping or falling off before the adhesive has dried, try that method. But if you feel safer with the finding in the sand, allow a few seconds longer under the broiler.

Finally, remember that the standard of jewelry you make rests entirely with you. If you use poor quality findings, chipped or poorly polished pebbles, and far too much adhesive, the end product will be junk! If you follow carefully the instructions set out above and use only your very best pebbles for jewelry-making, the end product will give you great pleasure for many years.

6. Where Do You Go From Here?

Future Collecting

Let's orient the many phases of the hobby at this point. Geology is the study of the earth's crust; the crust is composed of rocks and that division of geology is petrology. Rocks are composed of minerals. If you can polish a mineral, you have a gem. Someone who studies just gems, is, naturally, a gemologist. The person who polishes the mineral to make the gem is a lapidary. Well, sometimes a rock instead of a mineral is polished to make a gem; for example, unakite, which is made up of green epidote, gray quartz, and pink feldspar is a rock, not a mineral. It is really a granite, but it tumbles nicely.

So, when we go collecting, what are we? The word "rockhound" has become popular in the United States, but actually we are amateur mineral collectors. The professional is a mineralogist.

If you go past the pebble-collecting stage, you lose the family treasure-hunt image, and it becomes a serious business. You need hammers, splitting chisels, bull points (chisels that start cracks in rocks), pry bars, safety glasses, hard hats, and plenty of stamina. You need also a little knowledge of geology, of rock assemblages, and of mineral testing.

In view of the foregoing, it is suggested that your next step is to take the family to areas where fees are charged for collecting. These areas are accessible, reasonably safe, and the owner of the property will show you what to look for and where to dig. You need to bring your own digging tools. Here are several fee areas that will get you started.

NEW YORK: There are three fee areas for clear quartz crystals in the Mohawk Valley of New York. These crystals can be used in baroque jewelry just as they come out of the ground. The oldest hunting ground is near Middleville, New York, just south of the village, impossible to miss. The one north of Fonda, New York, is on Stone Arabia Road. Write Margaret Hastings, RD 1, Johnstown, New York, for further details, especially to find out when the snow departs in the spring. The newest one is at Crystal Grove Camp on the Lassellville Road about five miles north of St. Johnsville, New York.

ARIZONA: You cannot collect any petrified wood in the Petrified Forest. There are two ranches in Holbrook, Arizona, nearby that are open for a fee. They are: Do Bell Ranch, Box 26, Arizona 86025 and Greers Milky Ranch, Box 145, Arizona 86025.

IDAHO: Spencer Opal Mines, Mark Stetler, Box 113, Spencer, Idaho.

MAINE: Stop in to see Stan Perham at his store in West Paris, Maine 04289. Mr. Perham will give you free maps and information; you should wind up with tumbling-grade rose quartz at least. Most areas in Maine are free. There are some fee areas.

NEW MEXICO: Spanish Stirrup Ranch, Demming, 88030, for agate.

OHIO: For flint which tumbles nicely and for which Ohio is famous, the Neibarger Farm on Route 1, Box 57, and the Nethers Farm also on Route 1, both at Hopewell, 43746.

OREGON: There are a lot of agate fee areas in the state. Start with Prineville in the heart of the agate country. The city owns some agate claims that are free to tourists. Make further inquiries in Prineville.

SOUTH DAKOTA: The Flying U Ranch (the Bradfields) for agate and wood at Kadoka, 57543.

TEXAS: There are several agate locations at Alpine, Texas 79830. Among them, the Anderson Ranch, the Henderson Ranch, and the well known Woodward Ranch. Southwest Texas is agate country and there are many other fee areas there.

This is only a sampling of the areas selected on a regional basis that are open to collectors for a fee where collecting is possible and you do not have to worry. An informative, comprehensive article covering fee collecting areas and guided collecting was published in the June, 1971 issue of *The Lapidary Journal*. Back copies are usually available.

Planning a Trip

Write to everyone. Maybe half will reply, but you will have a start. Oregon is not the only state that gives the rock collector leads. The Geological Survey of the Maine Department of Economic Development at Augusta, Maine, publishes a pamphlet, "Maine Mineral Collecting." Another pamphlet on gem hunting is published by the Department of Recreation and Conservation, Parliament Buildings, Victoria, B.C., Canada. These are usually available from the tourist bureaus that welcome the visitor.

The Chamber of Commerce of the city of Marquette, Michigan, in a little tourist information book lists the names and addresses of the people who collect in that region. In Southern California the Imperial Valley Development Agency, P. O. Drawer, I.V., Imperial, California gives you leads at the county level.

Bancroft, Ontario, which holds an annual Gemboree, hands out a map of the mineralized areas at the tourist bureau. In Gouverneur, New York, a map of the minerals in the area is available in a local hardware store.

Pick out the area you want to visit and write to the Highway Departments, the Tourist Bureaus, and the Chambers of Commerce. Visit all the local rock shops. Howard Pearsons, who is a mineral and gem dealer at Monte Lake, British Columbia, puts out a book of maps called "B. C. Gem Trails." In addition, you can collect agates right next to his shop.

In the tumbling grade, nephrite jade from British Columbia and Wyoming is within reach of the average budget. Nephrite jade uses chrome oxide instead of cerium in the polishing phase. This means setting aside a barrel only for nephrite jade. If you visit B.C. or Wyoming, visit the local dealers to check. Finding nephrite jade in B.C. or Wyoming is not a family treasure hunt—you need to be equipped. If you are in Bancroft, Ontario, look at the local amazonite. For some reason it doesn't seem to get down into the United States.

There are good bargains in tumbling material at part-time dealers' on the West Coast. Their yards are loaded with local material they have collected themselves, and agates and petrified wood are unbelievably inexpensive. These dealers do not advertise in national magazines, but you can locate them in the little brochures you pick up at the highway stands that advertise tourist attractions.

It is more fun to find your own pebbles, tumble them to bring out the inner beauty, and then make your own jewelry. However, there is a lot of excellent tumbling material that is imported into the United States. Agates from Brazil are plentiful and inexpensive. Amethyst goes a little higher and good, dark, tumbling-grade material should wait until you know your way around the market place. Sodalite from Africa, and Brazil is inexpensive and good for tumbling. Rhodonite is another good stone for tumbling that won't break the budget. Malachite, while pretty, is a difficult mineral to polish. It is expensive and should be finished on chrome oxide which means perhaps setting aside a barrel only for malachite. Tiger's eye from South Africa will sell for a few dollars a pound with tumbling grade a little less.

Lapidary Suppliers

There are several hundred suppliers in the United States who serve the needs of the more than half a million people who pursue the related hobbies of tumbling, lapidary, jewelry and mineral collecting. To single out a few would be unfair. Following is a list of the magazines for the hobbyist; it is suggested that you subscribe to the magazine that covers the area you live in and get to know your local dealer. Some of the dealers put out tremendous catalogs which are yours for the asking. Others charge a nominal amount for a catalog. Large dealers in lapidary equipment and jewelry findings have free catalogs, many of which contain tips on cutting and polishing.

In tumbling, with which this book is principally concerned, grits are the single most important item. You should be able to locate easily a local supplier of silicon carbide grits anywhere in the United States. If you have trouble, the two large manufacturers in the United States are the Norton Company and the Carborundum Company, and to find your local supplier write to either the Electro Mineral Division of the Carborundum Co., P.O. Box 337, Niagara Falls, New York 14302, or to the Norton Company, New Bond Street, Worcester, Massachusetts 01606.

Magazines and Books

Magazines: There are three magazines that are specifically written for the amateur lapidary and mineral collector:

Earth Science
Box 550
Downers Grove, Illinois 60515

Gems and Minerals
P.O. Box 687
Mentone, California 92359

Rocks and Minerals
Box 29
Peekskill, New York

All are good magazines and, while national in scope, cater slightly to their particular region. *Earth Science* may stress fossils much more than the other two because the Midwest is rich in fossil locations.

Another magazine, *The Lapidary Journal,* is truly national in its content and as its cover indicates is for "Gem Cutters, Gem Collectors, and for Jewelers." The address is:

The Lapidary Journal
P.O. Box 80937
San Diego, California 92138.

All of them carry articles on collecting areas, cutting and polishing, jewelry-making, book reviews and where you can order the books you want, an up-to-date calendar of gem and mineral shows, and advertisements of all kinds including every tumbler on the market.

Books: After this book suggested for your transitional stage are:
"Discovering Rocks and Minerals"
(A Nature and Science Guide to Their
Collection and Identification)
by Ray A. Gallant and Christopher J. Schuberth
Natural History Press.

For an all-round book on lapidary:
"Gem Cutting: A Lapidary's Manual"
by John Sinkankas
Van Nostrand Reinhold Company.

For easy step-by-step approach to lapidary:
"Gem Cutting is Easy"
by Martin Walter
Crown Publishers, Inc.

To carry with you on field trips:
"A Field Guide to Rocks & Minerals"
by Dr. Frederick H. Pough
Houghton Mifflin Company.

There are scores of books on the market, but with the above you may never need to buy another book in your lifetime, but you will!

Mineral Shows

This is where you meet the people who advertise in the magazines and can shop around for findings, tumbling material, and equipment. There is usually a nominal admission charge. The sponsoring club and neighboring clubs will have a few exhibits, and if it is a large regional show, these exhibits may be competitive. For a beginner it is an eye-opener. Recently, local clubs are sponsoring open-air shows when the weather is favorable. Here, admission is free and the atmosphere informal, and besides selling there is swapping. There is not a weekend where two or three shows are not taking place in the United States, and no area of this country that does not see a mineral show once a year within an hour's drive of home.

A Final Word

Bear in mind that all property is owned or controlled by someone. On open public lands out west there are restrictions about taking out petrified wood. Even where permissible there are regulations on how much may be taken. Always be sure you have bona fide permission.

Respect private posted property even if you can see rubies and sapphires glistening in the sun. Get permission no matter how difficult it is or how time-consuming. A lack of courtesy may result in the closing of a good collecting area to all the hobbyists in the country.

Index